YA

P9-CFN-859

B   SUMMITVILLE   YOUNG ADULTS
MALCOLMBarr, Roger,
BAR   Malcolm X

SUMMITVILLE

NORTH MADISON COUNTY
PUBLIC LIBRARY SYSTEM
RALPH E. HAZELBAKER LIBRARY

THE IMPORTANCE OF

Malcolm X

These and other titles are included in The Importance Of biography series:

Cleopatra	Margaret Mead
Christopher Columbus	Michelangelo
Marie Curie	Wolfgang Amadeus Mozart
Thomas Edison	Napoleon Bonaparte
Albert Einstein	Richard M. Nixon
Benjamin Franklin	Jackie Robinson
Galileo Galilei	Anwar Sadat
Thomas Jefferson	Margaret Sanger
Chief Joseph	Mark Twain
Malcolm X	H.G. Wells

THE IMPORTANCE OF

Malcolm X

by
Roger Barr

Lucent Books, P.O. Box 289011, San Diego, CA 92198-9011

B
X, Malcolm
BAR

Library of Congress Cataloging-in-Publication Data

Barr, Roger, 1951–
    Malcolm X / by Roger Barr
        p.   cm.—(The Importance of)
    Includes bibliographical references and index.
    Summary: Describes the life of the controversial Black Mus-
lim leader, emphasizing his philosophies, goals, and legacy.
    ISBN 1-56006-044-1 (alk. paper)
    1. X, Malcolm, 1925–1965—Juvenile literature.   2. Black
Muslims—Biography—Juvenile literature.   3. Afro-Americans
—Biography—Juvenile literature.   [1. X, Malcolm, 1925–1965.
2. Afro-Americans—Biography.]   I. Title.   II. Series.
BP223.Z8L5717   1994
320.5'4'092—dc20   93-17853
[B]   CIP
                                                              AC

Copyright 1994 by Lucent Books, Inc., P.O. Box 289011, San
Diego, California, 92198-9011

No part of this book may be reproduced or used in any other
form or by any other means, electrical, mechanical, or otherwise, including, but not limited to photocopy, recording, or any
information storage and retrieval system, without prior written
permission from the publisher.

Contents

Important Dates in the Life of Malcolm X   6
Foreword   7

INTRODUCTION
"A Black Shining Prince"   8

CHAPTER 1
Young Malcolm Little   10

CHAPTER 2
Street Hustler   21

CHAPTER 3
From Malcolm Little to Malcolm X   32

CHAPTER 4
Minister Malcolm X   43

CHAPTER 5
A Split with Elijah Muhammad   59

CHAPTER 6
His Own Man   69

CHAPTER 7
The Assassination   80

CHAPTER 8
A Complex Legacy   91

Notes   101
For Further Reading   104
Works Consulted   105
Index   108
Credits   112
About the Author   112

NORTH MADISON COUNTY
PUBLIC LIBRARY SYSTEM
RALPH E. HAZELBAKER LIBRARY

Important Dates in the Life of Malcolm X

Malcolm Little is born to Earl and Louise Little in Omaha, Nebraska. Family later moves to Milwaukee, Wisconsin, then to Lansing, Michigan.	1925 / 1929	Family home is destroyed by mysterious fire.
	1931	Father, Earl Little, dies in streetcar mishap.
Mother, Louise Little, is declared insane, committed to state mental hospital, where she remains for twenty-six years.	1939 / 1941	Moves to Boston to live with his half-sister Ella. For next two years works at odd jobs and various hustles.
Visits Harlem in New York City.	1942	
While living in Boston, begins burglarizing houses with a group of friends.	1945 / 1946	Arrested January 12, 1946, and charged with several crimes; begins serving term at Charlestown State Prison.
Transferred to Concord Reformatory, he learns about Elijah Muhammad and converts to Islam.	1947 / 1952	Paroled from prison in Charlestown, moves to Detroit, Michigan; travels to Chicago and meets Elijah Muhammad.
Becomes first minister of New York City's Temple Number Seven after serving as assistant minister at Detroit and first minister at Boston temple.	1954 / 1958	Marries Betty X Sanders. Their marriage produces six children.
Silenced for ninety days by Elijah Muhammad after labeling President John F. Kennedy's assassination "the chickens coming home to roost."	1959 / 1963	New York City television series "The Hate That Hate Produced" introduces Nation of Islam and Malcolm X to general public.
Malcolm's house, owned by the Nation of Islam, is firebombed; Malcolm X assassinated at Harlem's Audubon Ballroom; publication of *The Autobiography of Malcolm X.*	1964 / 1965	Announces his departure from Nation of Islam. Four days later, announces formation of Muslim Mosque, Inc.; begins hajj to Mecca. During this trip, reverses his position on white people and takes the name El-Hajj Malik El-Shabazz; announces formation of Organization of Afro-American Unity.
Talmadge Hayer, Norman 3X Butler, and Thomas 15X Johnson convicted for the assassination of Malcolm X and receive life sentences.	1966	
	1992	*Malcolm X* debuts in American movie theaters.

Foreword

THE IMPORTANCE OF biography series deals with individuals who have made a unique contribution to history. The editors of the series have deliberately chosen to cast a wide net and include people from all fields of endeavor. Individuals from politics, music, art, literature, philosophy, science, sports, and religion are all represented. In addition, the editors did not restrict the series to individuals whose accomplishments have helped change the course of history. Of necessity, this criterion would have eliminated many whose contribution was great, though limited. Charles Darwin, for example, was responsible for radically altering the scientific view of the natural history of the world. His achievements continue to impact the study of science today. Others, such as Chief Joseph of the Nez Percé, played a pivotal role in the history of their own people. While Joseph's influence does not extend much beyond the Nez Percé, his nonviolent resistance to white expansion and his continuing role in protecting his tribe and his homeland remain an inspiration to all.

These biographies are more than factual chronicles. Each volume attempts to emphasize an individual's contributions both in his or her own time and for posterity. For example, the voyages of Christopher Columbus opened the way to European colonization of the New World. Unquestionably, his encounter with the New World brought monumental changes to both Europe and the Americas in his day. Today, however, the broader impact of Columbus's voyages is being critically scrutinized. *Christopher Columbus,* as well as every biography in The Importance Of series, includes and evaluates the most recent scholarship available on each subject.

Each author includes a wide variety of primary and secondary source quotations to document and substantiate his or her work. All quotes are footnoted to show readers exactly how and where biographers derive their information, as well as provide stepping stones to further research. These quotations enliven the text by giving readers eyewitness views of the life and times of each individual covered in The Importance Of series.

Finally, each volume is enhanced by photographs, bibliographies, chronologies, and comprehensive indexes. For both the casual reader and the student engaged in research, The Importance Of biographies will be a fascinating adventure into the lives of people who have helped shape humanity's past, present, and will continue to shape its future.

"A Black Shining Prince"

Although he stood in the glare of the national spotlight for only six years, Malcolm X is one of this century's most important figures in America's efforts to deal with racism. Born in 1925, Malcolm Little's early life mirrored the lives of millions of other people of color. He suffered from poverty and a broken home. As a teenager he fell into a life-style marked by various "hustles," drug use, and crime. Before he was twenty-one, he was sentenced to prison.

In prison, he reinvented himself, reading widely in history, religion, philosophy, and other subjects. Introduced by his family to the message of Elijah Muhammad, the founder of the Nation of Islam, he found truth in Muhammad's message that the white men were devils. He converted to Mr. Muhammad's version of Islam.

Upon his release from prison in 1952, Malcolm cast off what he considered as his slave name "Little" and replaced it with an "X," symbolizing his missing African name, stolen from his ancestors by white men. As the national spokesperson for the Nation of Islam, Malcolm X frequently described himself as "the angriest Negro in America," while spreading the Nation's "true knowledge" about the "devil white man" to black people.

Malcolm's message was a radical counterpoint to the message of Dr. Martin Luther King Jr., then the nation's most prominent civil rights leader. While Dr. King sought integration of blacks and whites through nonviolent methods, Malcolm preached separation from whites, and encouraged black people to use "any means necessary" to seize the rights they had been denied for more than 300 years. Viewed by many as a call to violence, Malcolm's message frightened many and some suggest it eventually played a significant

Malcolm X addresses the 1963 Black Muslim national convention. Born Malcolm Little, he rejected his last name because it was inherited from a white slave owner. He took the name X in place of his unknown African name.

Aware of the tradition of pride and self-respect begun by Malcolm X, African Americans demonstrate against racism.

role in pushing the nation toward adopting the more moderate proposals of Dr. King and other integrationists.

Different views on the Nation of Islam's role in the civil rights movement and an embarrassing scandal surrounding Elijah Muhammad forced Malcolm to break ties with the Nation in early 1964. Using a religious pilgrimage to Mecca, the holy city of the Islamic faith, as a new beginning, Malcolm modified his political position to accept the efforts of whites to help solve America's racial problem. He also sought to unite blacks in America and Africa in a common struggle against racism.

When he was assassinated on February 21, 1965, Malcolm was still struggling to redefine himself and turn his goals into a plan of action for black people. Yet his most important work might already have been done. Before Malcolm X, black people in America were called Negroes or worse. Malcolm popularized the term Afro-American. Many scholars credit him with helping to turn America's 22 million "Negroes" into "Afro-Americans" who were proud rather than ashamed of their black heritage. At Malcolm's funeral, actor Ossie Davis said "Malcolm was our manhood, our living, black manhood! This was his meaning to his people. And in honoring him, we honor the best in ourselves."[1]

Malcolm X's legacy lives on nearly three decades after his assassination. His *Autobiography of Malcolm X,* published months after his death, has become a classic. Both the book and the man remain an inspiration to millions of readers.

Although often overshadowed by Dr. Martin Luther King Jr., during his lifetime, Malcolm's popularity and influence have grown steadily since his death. An epic movie about his life introduced Malcolm X and his message to a new generation. A 1992 poll indicated that 84 percent of blacks between the ages of fifteen and twenty-four regard Malcolm X as a hero. His admirers continue to study his autobiography and speeches and to find new inspiration in them. His famous and often used phrase "by any means necessary" has been reinterpreted to include self-education and self-discipline. Snippets of Malcolm's speeches are included in the lyrics of many of today's rap songs.

Malcolm X will remain an important voice as long as racism divides America. His message is timeless. To each new generation of African Americans he will be, in the words of Ossie Davis, "a black shining Prince."[2]

1 Young Malcolm Little

When Malcolm Little was born in Omaha, Nebraska, on May 19, 1925, most Americans with white skin believed themselves superior to people with black skin. Growing up in a racist society, in which whites and blacks were prejudiced against each other had a dramatic effect on Malcolm's early life. He would also be shaped by the efforts of black people to break the bonds of racism. As an adult, Malcolm Little would recall both the events of his childhood and the history of an entire nation as he attempted to find solutions to the problem of racism.

Racism in America is older than the nation itself. In the 1600s shortly after the first Europeans settled in the New World in search of their own freedom, white slave traders journeyed to Africa, where they captured some black men and women and brought them to the New World to serve as slaves. Slaves were considered property and were bought and sold like horses.

Slavery had existed for more than a century when the American colonies revolted against England and won their independence in 1783. Slavery helped the new United States to grow, particularly the southern states, where slave labor was important to raising cotton.

Beginning in the early 1800s, slavery divided the nation: in the North, slavery was abolished, although black people hardly became the true equals of whites, but in the South, whites resisted efforts to end slavery because slave labor was vital to the region's cotton-based economy.

The slavery issue helped to plunge the nation into civil war late in April 1861. On

An advertisement for an upcoming slave auction in eighteenth-century America. Centuries of slavery generated a deep-seated racism in America that affected Malcolm at an early age.

TO BE SOLD, on board the
Ship *Bance-Island*, on tuefday the 6th
of *May* next, at *Afhley-Ferry*; a choice
cargo of about 250 fine healthy
NEGROES,
juft arrived from the
Windward & Rice Coaft.
—The utmoft care has
already been taken, and
fhall be continued, to keep them free from
the leaft danger of being infected with the
SMALL-POX, no boat having been on
board, and all other communication with
people from *Charles-Town* prevented.
Auftin, Laurens, & Appleby.

N. B. Full one Half of the above Negroes have had the
SMALL-POX in their own Country.

President Lincoln welcomed the new year of 1863 by signing the Emancipation Proclamation freeing all slaves in the Confederate states.

January 1, 1863, however, President Lincoln issued a proclamation that declared all slaves in the Confederate (southern) states to be free, "then, thenceforth, and forever." On April 9, 1865, the South surrendered to the North. With the surrender and the restoration of national unity, both the war and slavery in America officially ended.

Despite the official end of slavery, the United States remained a nation of contradictions. In 1866 the U.S. government passed its first civil rights act which guaranteed all Americans equal rights under law. But many whites, especially in the defeated South, refused to accept black people as equals. In 1867 a group of Tennessee whites formed an organization called the Ku Klux Klan to intimidate blacks who sought the rights granted them by law. Later, southern states passed "Jim Crow" laws which legally allowed the segregation or separation of blacks from whites.

African slaves toil in the cotton fields of the American South. Though equal by law, blacks have yet to be accepted as equals by many whites.

Through legislation and terrorism, blacks who lived in the South remained enslaved in everything but name. Although some black men and women were able to prosper, segregation kept most former slaves in poverty. They were forced to live in separate communities. They were denied good jobs, equal education, and the right to vote. They were refused service in public places. Blacks and whites could not even drink from the same water fountains.

In 1900 most black people lived in the rural South. But during the next twenty years, thousands fled the segregated South, moving to the industrialized cities in the northern states. There they hoped to find safety, better jobs, and better living conditions. But conditions in the North proved to be little better. Although the obvious signs of segregation did not exist, the North practiced its own subtle form of discrimination. Blacks remained second-class citizens.

Civil Rights Denied

The "chief aims" stated in the 1919 annual report of the National Association for the Advancement of Colored People (NAACP) were in effect a demand for the civil rights that were denied to black people around the time of Malcolm's birth.

"1. A vote for every Negro man and woman on the same terms as for white men and women.

2. An equal chance to acquire the kind of an education that will enable the Negro everywhere wisely to use this vote.

3. A fair trial in the courts for all crimes of which he is accused, by judges in whose election he has participated without discrimination because of race.

4. A right to sit upon the jury which passes judgment upon him.

5. Defense against lynching and burning at the hands of mobs.

6. Equal service on railroad and other public carriers. This to mean sleeping car service, dining car service, Pullman service, at the same cost and upon the same terms as other passengers.

7. Equal right to the use of public parks, libraries, and other community services for which he is taxed.

8. An equal chance for a livelihood in public and private employment.

9. The abolition of color-hyphenation and the substitution of 'straight Americanism.'"

Klansmen burn a cross during a demonstration. Still active today, the Ku Klux Klan was formed in 1867 to scare blacks out of demanding their civil rights.

The Little Family Saga

Among those who fled the South in search of a better life in the North was Earl Little, Malcolm's father. Born in Reynolds, Georgia, Earl Little grew up, married, and had three children. Later he left his wife and family behind and settled in Montreal, Canada. There he met Malcolm's mother, Louise, a native of the Caribbean island of Grenada. They were married on May 10, 1919. The Littles moved to Philadelphia, Pennsylvania, where they had three children.

Earl Little was a Baptist minister. Each Sunday he preached the Christian message to church members. But he was also interested in politics and the political and economic struggles of blacks. About this time, he became interested in the teachings of the black leader Marcus Garvey, the founder of the United Negro Improvement Association (UNIA). Garvey had founded UNIA after coming to the United States from the West Indies in 1916. Through UNIA, Garvey hoped to "improve the condition of the race."[3]

Although UNIA was one of numerous nationally known black organizations in America, Garvey's message to the nation's blacks was unique. Other black leaders believed that ending segregation, however long it took, was the answer to the nation's racial problem. Garvey believed separation of the races should be maintained. He believed that blacks should be proud of their color and of themselves, rather than accepting the belief of much of white society at the time that they were inferior.

The Complexity of Color

In Malcolm: The Life of a Man Who Changed Black America, *biographer Bruce Perry documents the complex role of color in Malcolm's relationship with his parents.*

"Malcolm's father was as dark as Malcolm was light. Though blacks who heard his crusading oratory thought he hated whites, [Earl Little's] white neighbors had a different impression. He greeted them with smiles and gave them fresh, homegrown produce from his vegetable garden. Black acquaintances recall how he shunned them for white ones whenever he found it expedient to do so. And the son he paraded when the church deacons visited him was Malcolm, his fair-skinned pride and joy. To the best of Malcolm's recollection, he was the only son his father ever took with him to the Garveyite gatherings where Earl vigorously championed the theme of black pride.

Malcolm's mother, whose American friends called her Louise, was also in conflict about color. Despite the way she extolled the ideal of black pride, she favored her lighter-skinned relatives and proudly insisted she was West Indian, not African-American. Her father, she said, was a white "prince" and a plantation owner. She tried to comb the natural curl from her hair in order to make it resemble the hair of the white friends she boasted. Sometimes she scrubbed Malcolm's face and neck violently. "I can make him look almost white if I bathe him enough," she told her white neighbor Anna Strohrer. Anna felt that Louise considered Malcolm superior to her other children because of his light complexion.

But Malcolm felt otherwise, partly because his mother bent over backward to make sure he would not think his fair skin made him superior. She admonished him to get out of the house so that the sun would tan and darken his skin. He thought she favored the darker children, partly because his light skin, like hers, was a painful reminder of her illegitimacy. He felt he was her least favorite child."

He taught that blacks should rely on themselves, owning their own land and their own businesses. Garvey's goal was for America's blacks to return to Africa and establish their own nation there. In their own nation, Garvey believed that "Negroes will be given the opportunity to develop by themselves." In 1922 Garvey offered the "true solution to the Negro problem."[4]

> We cannot allow a continuation of these crimes against our race. As four hundred million men, women, and children, worthy of the existence given us by the Divine Creator, we are determined to solve our problem, by redeeming our Motherland Africa from the hands of alien exploiters and founding there a government, a nation of our own, strong enough to lend protection to the members of our race scattered all over the world, and to compel the respect of nations and races of the earth.[5]

In the early 1920s, the Little family left Philadelphia and moved to Omaha, Nebraska. Earl Little took Garvey's nationalist message along with him. In Omaha, Earl Little became the head of the local chapter of Garvey's UNIA. In living rooms and kitchens, he preached Garvey's message.

The message was popular among Omaha's black residents, but not among its larger white population. Years later, in an interview with author Kenneth B. Clark, Malcolm recalled that "in those days . . . it wasn't the thing for a black man to be outspoken or to deviate from the accepted stereotype that was usually considered the right image for Negroes to fulfill or reflect . . . [and to discourage Earl Little from further preaching, whites] burned the house that we lived in."[6]

Malcolm also began his autobiography with an account of the conflict between his father and the area's white residents. In this version his father was away preaching in Milwaukee, Wisconsin, when the house was surrounded one night by hooded riders carrying shotguns and rifles. Malcolm recounted that the riders warned Louise that the Little family had better leave town, but he made no mention of the house being burned.

Although some scholars doubt that this incident ever occurred, the Little

Pleasant Grove Elementary School in Lansing, Michigan, was where Malcolm X first went to school. He was the only black student in his class.

family did leave Omaha shortly after Malcolm was born. They moved first to Milwaukee, and then to Lansing, Michigan, early in 1928. In Lansing they purchased a house. Earl continued his Baptist ministry and his work for UNIA.

In Lansing, the Little family ran into trouble again. In September 1929, they were notified that the deed to their house included a stipulation that the land "shall never be rented, leased, sold to, or occupied . . . by persons other than those of the Caucasian race."[7]

A nearby white land developer believed that the property values would decrease with a black family living in the neighborhood. He convinced the former owner of the Littles' house to cooperate in an effort to evict the Little family. A lawsuit was filed, and the court ordered the Little family to leave the home they had purchased.

On the night of November 7, before the Little family moved, the house caught fire. At the time, Malcolm was only four years old. The family blamed the fire on local white people who did not like Earl Little's black nationalist preaching. As an adult Malcolm referred to the incident in an interview, noting that his father "was a clergyman, a Christian, and it was Christians who burned the house . . . people who teach . . . brotherhood and all that".[8]

But in 1929 Earl Little himself was suspected of starting the fire. He was questioned by police, who believed he set the fire to avenge the family's eviction. Earl Little was charged with arson, but the charges were dropped several months later. The identity of the person or persons who set the fire has never been conclusively proved.

After the fire, Earl Little built a new house in Lansing. But times were very

Marcus Garvey headed the United Negro Improvement Association, which promoted self-determination and pride among African Americans. Malcolm's father was an active UNIA leader.

hard. The Little family now numbered seven children: Hilda, Philbert, Malcolm, Reginald, Wilfred, Yvonne, and Wesley. The family lived on what they grew in their garden, collections from Earl's preaching, and the odd jobs he did. Malcolm and his brothers and sisters were often hungry. The house was filled with tension because Earl and Louise quarreled frequently. Both parents were severe disciplinarians and often beat their children.

On September 28, 1931, tragedy struck the Little family again. After an argument with Louise, Earl stalked out of the house. As he left, Louise experienced a vision that he would not return and begged him not to go. Later that night, Earl Little was found injured on the street. He had been run over by a streetcar. He lived for about two hours. Malcolm recalled learning of his father's death:

> I remember waking up to the sound of my mother's screaming again. When I scrambled out, I saw the police in the living room; they were trying to calm her down. She had snatched on her clothes to go with them. And all of us children who were staring knew without anyone having to say it that something terrible had happened to our father. . . . It was morning when we children at home got the word that he was dead. I was six.[9]

Controversy still surrounds Earl Little's death. Official records indicate the fatal injuries were accidental. According to one historian, Earl was conscious when found and admitted having missed the step and

fallen beneath the wheels of the streetcar. However, Malcolm's mother believed that her husband had died at the hands of whites who opposed his views on black nationalism. As a boy, Malcolm remained uncertain about how his father died. By the time he became an adult, he had accepted his mother's version of the story.

Hard Times

After Earl's death, the Little family suffered even harder times. Louise bought groceries on credit. Although she hated to, she was forced to accept welfare to feed Malcolm and his brothers and sisters.

By 1934, the Little family's situation was growing desperate. It was perhaps the worst year of the Great Depression and many families, white and black, did not have enough to eat. The Little family,

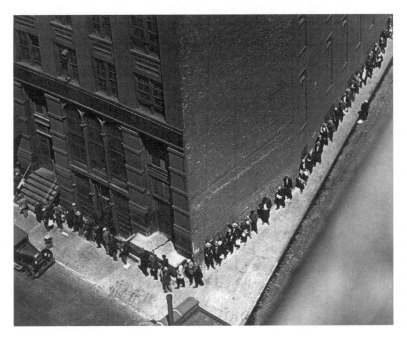

Impoverished and hungry, unemployed Americans wait in a bread line during the Great Depression. Malcolm X recalled being so hungry during this time that he was dizzy.

A Tough Childhood

In 1963 Malcolm X described his childhood to Alex Haley in an interview published in the June issue of Playboy *magazine.*

"I was born in Omaha on May 19, 1925. My light color is the result of my mother's mother having been raped by a white man. I hate every drop of white blood in me. Before I am indicted for hate again, sir—is it wrong to hate the blood of a rapist? But to continue: My father was a militant follower of Marcus Garvey's 'Back to Africa' movement. The Lansing, Michigan, equivalent of the Ku Klux Klan warned him to stop preaching Garvey's message, but he kept on, and one of my earliest memories is of being snatched awake one night with a lot of screaming going on because our home was afire. But my father got louder about Garvey, and the next time he was found bludgeoned in the head, lying across the streetcar tracks. He died soon and our family was in a bad way. We were so hungry we were dizzy and we had nowhere to turn. Finally the authorities came in and we children were scattered about in different places as public wards. I happened to become the ward of a white couple who ran a correctional school for white boys. This family liked me in the way they liked their house pets."

Malcolm recalled years later, lived mainly on its pride. Family friends sometimes visited the Littles, bringing food, which Louise accepted even though she considered it charity. Sometimes food was so scarce that Louise picked dandelion greens and boiled them in a pot. "We were so hungry we were dizzy and we had nowhere to turn," Malcolm recalled many years later.[10]

During that hard year, however, even the family's pride began to erode and the family started to come apart. For the next few years Louise Little grew less and less able to care for everyone. Malcolm had mixed feelings about remaining in the house. It was home, but there was hardly anything to make him happy there. He did poorly in school and was suspended frequently for bad behavior. Now entering his teens, he spent little time at home. After being permanently suspended from the seventh grade, he boarded across town with a family named Gohanna so he could continue his education by attending another school. Although the arrangement between the Little and Gohanna families was strictly financial and only temporary, it made its mark on Malcolm. As an adult, Malcolm claimed the time spent with the Gohannas was the beginning of the state's attempt to break up the family.

Although in fact the state had made no deliberate effort to break up the Little family, their condition went from bad to worse. After years of struggle, Louise suffered a complete mental breakdown. On January 9, 1939, she was judged insane and institutionalized in Kalamazoo, Michigan, where she remained for twenty-six years until her release in 1965.

At the age of fourteen, Malcolm was made a ward of the court and placed in a juvenile home in the nearby town of Mason. Malcolm went willingly. The home, run by Mrs. Swerlein, a large, friendly white woman, was more stable than any environment Malcolm had experienced in years.

Malcolm began the eighth grade in Mason. For a time, he seemed to do better. He was one of the more popular students in his class. In the second semester, he was elected class president. But in the spring of 1939 an incident occurred that soured Malcolm on school once again. In a conversation with one of his teachers, Malcolm expressed his interest in becoming a lawyer. The teacher, although sympathetic, gave Malcolm what he thought was good advice. He told Malcolm he should instead consider carpentry, because becoming a lawyer was not a realistic career goal for a "nigger."

While he lived in the juvenile home, Malcolm spent his weekdays in the white world of Mason and his weekends with his brothers and sisters who still lived in the family home in the black section of Lansing. Biographer Bruce Perry describes Malcolm as a "chameleon" who tried to fit in both places, but in reality did not fit in either place. In Mason,

when anything was stolen at school, [Malcolm] was the first to be questioned. To get a haircut he either had to patronize the local barber shops after hours, or take a bus into Lansing. Older boys "accidentally" elbowed him as he passed by. Even the Swerleins called him a "nigger." . . . He was no more accepted by Lansing's blacks than by Mason's whites. At West Side parties, he stood around, watching others jitterbug, bob for apples, or spin the bottle. He was always on the edge of the crowd, a lonely looking incommunicative, forgotten youngster.[11]

A Way Out

In the fall of 1939, Malcolm and his brothers and sisters were visited by their half-sister from Boston, Ella Little, a grown daughter from Earl Little's first marriage. Malcolm was impressed by Ella's confidence and her attitude about herself. She was the first black woman he had ever met who was proud of her dark skin.

Ella's visit was Malcolm's first connection to a different life. In the summer of 1940, he caught a bus to Boston to visit her. Malcolm was awed by the neon lights, pool halls, night clubs, and flashy cars. He was thrilled by the music he heard at the Roseland State Ballroom. He attended a black church where members of the congregation threw their bodies and souls into worship. And for the first time, he saw black-white couples strolling down the street arm in arm.

Malcolm returned to Michigan, but the visit to Boston had changed him. He

NORTH MADISON COUNTY
PUBLIC LIBRARY SYSTEM
RALPH E. HAZELBAKER LIBRARY

A Turning Point

In his Autobiography, *Malcolm recalled some advice from a teacher that betrayed the innate prejudices of white people. Malcolm called this incident the "first major turning point" in his life.*

"I know that he probably meant well in what he happened to advise me that day. I doubt that he meant any harm. It was just in his nature as an American white man. I was one of his top students, one of the school's top students—but all he could see for me was the kind of future 'in your place' that almost all white people see for black people.

He told me, 'Malcolm, you ought to be thinking about a career. Have you been giving it thought?'

The truth is, I hadn't. I never have figured out why I told him, 'Well, yes, sir, I've been thinking I'd like to be a lawyer.' Lansing certainly had no Negro lawyers—or doctors either—in those days, to hold up an image I might have aspired to. All I really knew for certain was that a lawyer didn't wash dishes, as I was doing.

Mr. Ostrowski looked surprised, I remember, and leaned back in his chair and clasped his hands behind his head. He kind of half-smiled and said, 'Malcolm, one of life's first needs is for us to be realistic. Don't misunderstand me now. We all here like you, you know that. But you've got to be realistic about being a nigger. A lawyer—that's no realistic goal for a nigger. You need to think about something you *can* be. You're good with your hands—making things. Everybody admires your carpentry shop work. Why don't you plan on carpentry? People like you as a person—you'd get all kinds of work.'"

thought constantly about the sights and sounds of Boston. But there was something else about his Boston visit that haunted Malcolm as he wandered around Lansing. Years later he realized that for the first time in his life, he had been in a large mass of people who had the same color skin as he.

For Malcolm, Boston soon came to represent a way out of his difficult, unhappy life in Michigan. He asked Ella if he could come and live with her, and she arranged for him to move to Boston. In February 1941, Malcolm once again boarded the bus for Boston, grateful to put his life in Michigan behind him.

2 Street Hustler

From the moment Malcolm arrived in Boston a few months short of his sixteenth birthday, he was mostly on his own. For the next six years of his life, he alternated between trying to live as a legitimate citizen and being a street hustler—using and selling drugs, committing robberies, and participating in illegal gambling, bootlegging, and prostitution. Throughout these years, he wandered restlessly between Michigan, Boston, and New York's Harlem. His wandering came to an end when he was sent to prison.

There has been much discussion and speculation about Malcolm's six-year career as a street hustler and criminal. Malcolm himself contributed to the confusion of what is factual and what is fiction. His autobiography, which contains a detailed account of his career as an addict, pusher, pimp, gambler, armed robber, and burglar, remains the major source of information about this period of his life. However, the book must be read with some caution. Numerous characters are composites of real people Malcolm knew. Others have different names. Researchers also have determined that Malcolm exaggerated some of his criminal behavior, while leaving out certain important incidents entirely. Biographer Bruce Perry attributes these exaggerations to Malcolm's desire to use himself as an example of someone who had escaped the ghetto and turned his life around.

Years later, after his religious conversion . . . he'd emphatically deny that he had been trying to exaggerate his "sordid" past. But the villainous image he projected enabled him to transform youthful failure into felonious success. By exaggerating how bad he had been, he was able to portray himself as a living symbol of moral uplift, an inspiring example of how wrongdoers could "clean themselves up" and reform themselves.[12]

Some details may have been omitted from the autobiography to avoid repetition. Perry believes that other details about his early life and his criminal career were excluded because the memories were painful to the adult Malcolm. Some information was left out because it did not fit the image of himself that Malcolm attempted to create in his autobiography.

The exact details of Malcolm's career as a street hustler and criminal worry some leaders of today's black communities who fear that black men and women use Malcolm's criminal career to justify their own criminal behavior. For that reason, Malcolm's criminal past and the ways he dealt with it continue to be discussed and examined.

A Rebellion Against Childhood

In Malcolm: The Life of a Man Who Changed Black America, *author Bruce Perry links Malcolm's criminal behavior with rebellion against his childhood.*

"The criminal Malcolm wielded power over his luckless victims, just as those who had tyrannized him had wielded power over him. He forced his way into locked homes the way a valiant knight might storm a castle. Perhaps he feared the barriers he breached much less than he feared the barriers to the success and acceptance he longed for.

He rebelled against civil authority with a fervor stemming from earlier, unresolved battles against parental and pedagogical authority. If he could not master the law one way, perhaps he could do it another. He preferred to be bad rather than an acknowledged failure, and to be condemned by society at large rather than by taskmasters at home and school. The criminal Malcolm was simultaneously a repudiation of everything his father and Ella wanted him to be and an affirmation of everything they were."

Homeboy

Years later Malcolm compared his hicklike appearance upon his arrival in Boston to the comic strip character Little Abner. His reddish hair was cut country style and his green suit was too small to cover his lanky frame.

Ella lived in Boston's black neighborhood in the more exclusive Waumbeck and Humboldt Avenue hill district. Ella was financially well off, and she had affluent neighbors. At first Malcolm was awed by the black residents of the hill district. He thought they were high class and well educated, working in important jobs. But his awe soon disappeared, and he decided that with one difference, the hill district blacks were only big-city versions of the blacks he had known back in Michigan. The difference, Malcolm observed, was that Boston's hill district blacks fooled themselves into believing they were more cultured, more important than the black residents who lived in Roxbury, the nearby ghetto section. To Malcolm, Ella's black neighbors were pretentious and trying to act white.

Ella proved to be demanding and strict. She wanted Malcolm to fit into her life-style, but he rebelled. Despite her disapproval, he soon started hanging out in Roxbury. With the blacks of the ghetto, in the pool halls and nightclubs that had captivated

Boston's black ghetto was in the city's Roxbury district. Young Malcolm liked to hang out in Roxbury's pool halls and nightclubs.

him during his earlier visit to Boston, Malcolm felt more comfortable.

In the ghetto, he met another young black man he called Shorty in his autobiography. In reality Shorty was a composite of several people Malcolm knew in Boston, including a young man named Malcolm Jarvis. Jarvis, too, was from Lansing and the two teenagers quickly struck up a friendship. Jarvis called Malcolm "Homeboy."

Through Jarvis, Malcolm received his real introduction to the ghetto culture. He drank his first liquor, smoked his first cigarettes and his first "reefers." He shot craps and started betting a dollar a day on the "numbers," an illegal lottery.

Jarvis also helped Malcolm get a "slave"—a job at the Roseland Ballroom, where the big bands and swing bands played. Malcolm was trained as a shoeshine boy by Freddie, a black man who had won big on the numbers and was leaving. Freddie showed Malcolm the mechanics of shining shoes and delivered some final ad-

vice: "The main thing you got to remember is that everything in the world is a hustle."[13] It was advice that Malcolm would follow for the next six years.

Malcolm sometimes shined the shoes of the musicians who played the Roseland. He later claimed to have been close friends with many of his musician customers, a claim disputed by researchers. Malcolm soon learned that the shoeshine job had less to do with shining shoes than with providing illegal services for the Roseland's mostly white customers. He bought condoms and resold them at a higher price. He sold liquor and marijuana. He steered white men toward black prostitutes. For these services, Malcolm received generous tips.

Fitting In

Malcolm quickly shed his "Little Abner" image. When he learned that he could obtain clothing on credit, he went out and bought a zoot suit, the fashion statement of the day. A salesman showed him a sky blue zoot and Malcolm tried it on. The pants flared to thirty inches at his knees, then narrowed to twelve inches at his ankles. The coat was tight at his waist and flared out at the bottom. As a gift, the

---

A Step Toward Self-Degradation

A passage in Malcolm's Autobiography *describes the process of getting a conk to make his hair look like a white man's, and his later realization that the conk was a symbol of self-degradation.*

"The congolene [a homemade mixture of lye, potatoes, and eggs] just felt warm when Shorty started combing it in. But then my head caught fire.

I gritted my teeth and tried to pull the sides of the kitchen table together. The comb felt as if it was raking my skin off.

My eyes watered, my nose was running, I couldn't stand it any longer; I bolted to the washbasin. I was cursing Shorty with every name I could think of when he got the spray going and started soap-lathering my head. . . .

When Shorty let me stand up and see in the mirror, my hair hung down in limp, damp strings. My scalp still flamed, but not as badly; I could bear it. He draped the towel around my shoulders, over my rubber apron, and began again vaselining my hair. . . .

My first view in the mirror blotted out the hurting. I'd seen some pretty conks, but when it's the first time, on your *own* head, the transformation, after the lifetime of kinks, is staggering. . . .

How ridiculous I was! Stupid enough to stand there simply lost in admiration of my hair now looking 'white,' reflected in the mirror in Shorty's room. . . .

This was my first really big step toward self-degradation: when I endured all of that pain, literally burning my flesh with lye, in order to cook my natural hair until it was limp, to have it look like a white man's hair. I had joined that multitude of Negro men and women in America who are brainwashed into believing that the black people are 'inferior'—and white people 'superior'—that they will even violate and mutilate their God-created bodies to try to look 'pretty' by white standards."

When Malcolm's hair grew long enough, he got his first "conk" to straighten the kinks out and make his hair look more like a white man's. When the fiery process was finished, Malcolm looked into the mirror. The kinks were gone. His red hair was slick and straight, like a white man's. Admiring his new look, Malcolm vowed never to give up his conk. For years he regularly submitted himself to the painful process. Years later, however, Malcolm regarded the conk as "the emblem of [the black man's] shame that he is black."[14]

Malcolm soon left his job at the Roseland Ballroom because he hated to shine shoes while everyone else danced. He took a job as a soda jerk in a drugstore. There, he met a girl he called Laura in his autobiography. Ella approved of Laura, but the relationship did not last long. At the Roseland one night with Laura, Malcolm met a white girl he called Sophia in his autobiography. Malcolm soon abandoned Laura for Sophia. For the black men of the ghetto, having a white girl friend was a status symbol. Malcolm paraded Sophia around the neighborhood, apparently unaware that he was lapsing into some behavior he criticized in Ella's neighbors.

Malcolm maintained his relationship with Sophia even after she married another man. A few years later, Sophia would play a major role in his life.

Harlem Hustler

The country's entry into World War II late in 1941 took men out of the work force and put them into the armed services. For those left behind or too young to serve, as Malcolm was at the time, jobs were easy to

A man sports a "zoot suit," the "in" thing to wear in the 1940s black subculture. Malcolm X wore one during his hustler days in Boston and New York.

salesman presented Malcolm with a narrow leather belt with the initial "L" on it, and a long gold-plated chain. To complete the new outfit, Malcolm bought a blue hat with a feather sticking out beyond the wide brim.

find. By lying about his age, Malcolm was able to get a job with the railroad as fourth cook, a glorified name for dishwasher. He soon left the railroad but returned in January 1942, lured by the opportunity to replace the sandwich man on the Yankee Clipper, a train that ran between Boston and New York. Malcolm took the job because he wanted to see New York City, and Harlem, the black community of New York.

Harlem made an immediate and permanent impression on Malcolm. "That's where I saw in the bars all these men and women with what looked like the easiest life in the world. Plenty of money, big cars, all of it," he recalled years later.[15] In a nightclub called Small's Paradise, Malcolm was fascinated by the conservatively dressed black men, who sat drinking and talking quietly among themselves. Almost instantly he abandoned his Boston life and became a Harlemite.

Small's Paradise quickly became Malcolm's headquarters in Harlem. Although Harlem was an impoverished ghetto, it was also the center of black culture. Emerging black writers lived there alongside the street hustlers. Many famous black musicians either lived in Harlem or frequently played in the local clubs. For these reasons, Harlem was "seventh heaven" to the young Malcolm. Being tall, he was able to pass for an adult and to gain entry into any nightclub or bar. He patronized Small's Paradise and the Braddock Bar so often that the bartenders began to pour his favorite drink when they saw him walk through the door. In both bars, the customers started calling Malcolm "Red," in reference to the color of his hair. Because

Harlem residents in the 1940s sport the latest fashions on their way to one of the area's well-known night spots. This was the world of the teenage Malcolm X.

Patrons crowd the dance floor at Small's Paradise in 1940s Harlem. As a waiter at Small's, Malcolm learned the hustlers' tricks of the trade.

he later told people he was from Detroit, Michigan, he eventually became known as Detroit Red to distinguish him from other red-haired street hustlers. One of his fellow hustlers became famous as Red Foxx, the popular comedian and actor.

Through most of 1942, Malcolm worked for the railroad, spending as much time as he could in Harlem. In October, he returned to Michigan to visit members of his family, but by March 1943, he was back working for the railroad. Shortly after his return, he was fired after a passenger complained about him. He settled in Harlem and took a job at Small's Paradise.

Malcolm waited on tables and did other odd jobs at Small's, glad to be a part of the Harlem scene. He met an assortment of hustlers who bore exotic nicknames: "Cadillac" Drake and Sammy the Pimp, Dollarbill, Fewclothes, and Jumpsteady. From these and others, Malcolm learned the hustling society's first rule:

never trust anyone but your close friends, and select your friends carefully. For Malcolm, it was easy advice to follow: He had grown up not trusting many people. Years later, Malcolm understood the circumstance that brought the hustlers together.

> Many times since, I have thought about it, and what it really meant. In one sense, we were huddled in there, bonded together in seeking security and warmth and comfort from each other, and we didn't know it. All of us—who might have probed space, or cured cancer, or built industries—were, instead, black victims of the white man's American social system.[16]

Exiled from Paradise

Although Small's Paradise had become the center of Malcolm's world, he soon

Young ladies at the bar in Small's Paradise. Malcolm was fired from Small's when he arranged for a prostitute to meet an undercover policeman.

made the mistake of violating Small's strictest rule. The management had forbidden the staff from steering U.S. servicemen toward any vices. When Malcolm attempted to arrange for an undercover policeman to meet a prostitute, he was not only fired, but also banned from Small's Paradise.

For a brief time, Malcolm became a small-time drug dealer, selling marijuana in the streets. In August 1943 he signed on with the New York Central Railroad but was fired only two months later. He applied for work at the Seaboard Railroad in February 1944, but left in less than a month.

For the rest of 1944, Malcolm worked a variety of illegal and legitimate jobs. Using the identification cards of the various railroads he had worked for, Malcolm was

able to travel around the Northeast free of charge. For a few months, he followed the musicians he knew and liked from town to town, supplying them with marijuana. He smoked marijuana himself and also used cocaine. How dependent he became on drugs is sometimes debated, but Malcolm later described himself as an addict.

On occasion, Malcolm committed small robberies to obtain money to live on. It was risky, but Malcolm had become adjusted to the hustler's life. He had no skills for legitimate work. He considered himself smart enough to live by his wits, preying on others.

To protect himself, Malcolm carried a small handgun tucked into the waistband of his pants at the small of his back, a spot police officers never searched when they stopped and frisked him.

His career as a traveling drug dealer soon ended. Between July and September 1944, Malcolm worked as a bar entertainer at the Lobster Pond in Harlem. Using the name Jack Carlton, Malcolm danced for the Lobster Pond's customers and sometimes played the drums with other would-be musicians. In October, he left New York and returned to Boston, where he worked for three weeks as a packer at the Sears & Roebuck store in nearby Brookline.

In late November 1944, Malcolm got into trouble. He stole a fur coat that belonged to Ella's sister Grace. Grace had Malcolm arrested, and he received a three-month suspended jail sentence, plus a year of probation.

He returned to Michigan in March 1945, where his troubles with the law continued. He worked briefly as a waiter and busboy, but also committed several robberies. Again he was arrested but his trial was postponed. He took a short-lived job in a Lansing mattress factory, then worked for five days sweeping floors in the Reo automobile factory.

In August of that year, he returned to Harlem. Before long, he began hauling bootlegged whiskey. The illegal job ended quickly, however, when his employer suddenly disappeared, never to be heard from again.

The hustler's life-style began to take its toll on Malcolm, who was still in his teens. He was looking over his shoulder all the time. Years later, he understood that the life he was experiencing was no real life at all. Nearly two decades later, as he dictated his autobiography, Malcolm wondered how he survived his life on the street. What had once impressed him as the "easiest life in the world" he recognized as a kind of death. "Through all of this time of my life, I really was dead—mentally dead. I just didn't know that I was."[17]

Run Out of Harlem

In the fall of 1945 a conflict with another Harlem hustler named West Indian Archie nearly cost Malcolm his life. Malcolm had put money on several lottery numbers through Archie. That is, he had grouped the numbers in different combinations to increase his chances of "hitting" or winning. On this occasion Malcolm claimed to have combined a certain set of winning numbers. Archie never carried written records, for safety's sake, in case he was arrested, and paid Malcolm his winnings on the spot. But later, after checking his written betting slips, Archie discovered that he had written down numbers different from the ones Malcolm had claimed.

One of them had made a simple mistake, but neither would admit the error. Money was less the issue than pride and reputation. Neither hustler could afford to be bullied by the other and have his street reputation tarnished. Then everyone would try to bully the loser. Carrying a gun, Archie confronted Malcolm inside a bar, but other customers distracted Archie long enough for Malcolm to make a dignified exit.

His escape was only temporary. Archie would surely come looking for him. There would be a gunfight, and one of them would be wounded or killed. Just when Malcolm felt that everything was closing in on him, a fellow hustler called Malcolm's

A Dangerous Role Model?

In "The Autobiography of Deidre Bailey: Thoughts on Malcolm X and Black Youth," Deidre Bailey points out that Malcolm's career as a street hustler serves as a dangerous model to blacks. This essay appears in Malcolm X: In Our Own Image, *edited by Joe Wood.*

"Malcolm obviously serves as a role model first to black men. Just like what Malcolm went through—drug dealing, pimping, stealing, robbing—that's what so many of our black men are doing now. They look at Malcolm and they can relate to his life. A sense of wanting to get out but also of feeling trapped in a society that has offered no other alternative but to turn to the streets. 'How can I get out of this? How can I be successful without doing this?' These are the dilemmas that young black men are faced with today. The main thing is they want to be successful. Unfortunately, the only means that many see is through selling drugs. They say, 'Hey, Malcolm sold drugs, I sold drugs. He pimped for a living, I had to pimp for a living. He was in jail. I was in jail.' They use Malcolm as a justification. These are the guys who are not ready to get out of it. They feel like they're living too well at this time. In effect they are living out the American Dream. . . . Still, some of the dealers also say, 'Okay, this is my situation now, this was Malcolm's situation at one point, too. He was able to get out of it, I have hopes of getting out of it also.' For a lot of them, though, the time is probably never going to be right. And they'll just end up either dying young or in prison."

Three black males are arrested for dealing drugs.

friend Malcolm Jarvis in Boston. Jarvis drove to Harlem, and Malcolm went back to Boston with him, leaving Harlem behind. He would not see the streets of Harlem again for almost a decade.

Caught

Leaving Harlem had saved Malcolm from a certain and perhaps fatal confrontation with West Indian Archie. But returning to Boston did not save Malcolm from himself. After a month of doing nothing, Malcolm decided it was time for a new hustle. He settled on house burglary and put together a gang of friends. The group included Malcolm himself, his friend Malcolm Jarvis, a friend of Jarvis's, and two white women—Malcolm's old girlfriend Sophia and her sister.

The burglary ring operated through the holiday season of 1945 and into the new year. The sisters scouted the wealthy white neighborhoods, posing as saleswomen or poll takers. They identified the houses with valuables and explained the layout. The men then committed the burglaries. The stolen items were sold at a fraction of their worth to a middleman known as a fence.

The operation continued until Malcolm pawned a wedding ring that could easily be identified, leaving a stolen watch for repair in the same jewelry store. He gave his own name and his sister Ella's address to the jeweler. No experienced hustler would have made these mistakes. Subconsciously, Malcolm seemed to be inviting capture.

When he returned to pick up the watch on January 12, 1946, the police were waiting. A single detective ordered him into the store. As they moved toward the back, another black man stepped into the store, distracting the detective. Malcolm had a chance to draw his gun and shoot, but for reasons he later attributed to God, he chose to surrender instead. It was a wise decision, for two more detectives were hiding in the back room. Had Malcolm tried to run, he might have been shot and killed. He was arrested, and the other members of the burglary ring were soon taken into custody.

Although Malcolm had been lucky for six years, surviving scrapes with hustlers and arrests for various crimes, his luck had finally run out. Malcolm and his friend Jarvis interpreted their high bail as punishment for their association with white women. While Sophia and her sister were released on low bail, bail was set at $10,000 for Malcolm and Jarvis.

The high bail was only a prelude. At their sentencing during February 1946, the entire weight of the justice system came down on them. Malcolm and Jarvis appeared in court for sentencing on fourteen counts of burglary. Jarvis was sentenced first. As each of the fourteen charges was read, the judge sentenced Jarvis eight to ten years in prison. The judge finally said that the sentences were to run "concurrently." Jarvis nearly collapsed, not knowing that the word meant that all the sentences would be served at the same time.

Malcolm was sentenced to ten years in prison. He was three months short of his twenty-first birthday. He entered prison on February 27, 1946, angry for reasons he could not put into words and still mentally dead.

Chapter

3 From Malcolm Little to Malcolm X

Malcolm Little spent a grim period becoming acclimated to the nearly 150-year-old Charlestown State Prison. In his autobiography, Malcolm recalled his difficult first days as a convict. He was broken and alone in a strange and hostile environment. In the street, he had used drugs frequently to help him escape the pain of his life. Now he was suddenly without drugs.

As a new prisoner or "fish," he was physically sick and ill-tempered. His cell was so small that he could lie on his cot and touch both walls. Day after day he sat in the cramped cell, the smell of the covered pail that served as his toilet filling his nostrils.

With money supplied by his sister Ella, he was able to illegally purchase quantities

The state prison at Charlestown, Massachusetts, became Malcolm's home on February 27, 1946.

A Picture of Prison Life

Biographer Bruce Perry draws an alternative picture of Malcolm's early prison life in Malcolm: The Life of a Man Who Changed Black America.

"Malcolm's hostility toward religion prompted most of the men in his cellblock to call him Satan. He seemed to relish his devilish image, which attracted attention and enhanced his status the way his sinful image had enhanced his status on the streets. Years later, Malcolm would portray himself as a tough, refractory convict who had refused to respond when his prison number was called, dropped his dishes in the dining hall, cursed his guards, and spent considerable time in solitary confinement. But prisoners were addressed by name, not by number. There was no dining hall at Charlestown; each inmate ate locked in his cell. Malcolm's voluminous prison record contains no evidence that he cursed any guards or spent more than his first day in prison in solitary confinement. Nor do any of the officers or guards who were later interviewed recall him doing so. They were well briefed about which inmates cause trouble. They had to be for their own protection."

of nutmeg from the prison guards. The kitchen spice gave him a "buzz," a very poor substitute for the drug highs he was used to.

Convicts sometimes turn to religion. While Malcolm was in prison, however, he turned his back completely on religion. He called the prison chaplain names and went on such tirades against God and the Bible that he earned a new nickname from his fellow convicts. They called him Satan.

As the days melted into weeks, then months, Malcolm began to take notice of a man he called Bimbi in his autobiography. Bimbi stood apart from the other black convicts. He would not respond to the street language they used. He was well read on many subjects. Malcolm noticed that inmates and guards alike listened as Bimbi talked for hours about history and religion. Malcolm realized that his fellow convict was able to command the attention and respect of everyone by using words. In his autobiography, Malcolm described Bimbi as the first person he had ever met who could capture and hold the admiration of people through what he said. The description seemed to ignore Malcolm's father, Earl Little, who undoubtedly moved people with his preaching.

One day Bimbi told Malcolm that he "had some brains" if he would use them and urged Malcolm to take advantage of the prison library and correspondence courses. Malcolm had figured he was through with formal education when he finished the eighth grade. Whatever he had learned in school, he had forgotten during his years on the street. But with time weighing heavily on his hands, and perhaps to gain some of the respect that Bimbi had, he began a correspondence course in English. He began to request books whose titles sounded interesting from the prison library.

The Natural Religion

In January 1947, Malcolm was transferred to another prison in Massachusetts, the Concord Reformatory. While at Concord, Malcolm received a letter from his brother Philbert, who wrote that he had discovered the "natural religion" for black people. He told Malcolm that he had become a member of the Nation of Islam and instructed Malcolm to "pray to Allah" for deliverance.

Malcolm's grammar skills had improved through his studies, but his attitude about religion had remained the same. Writing more clearly and legibly than when he first entered prison, he sent Philbert a nasty reply.

Malcolm soon received a letter from another brother, Reginald, filled with family news. Reginald also instructed Malcolm not to eat pork or smoke cigarettes. If he mastered these disciplines, Reginald promised to show him how to get out of prison. Although Malcolm did not connect the two

letters, they were part of a campaign mounted by his family to get him to convert to the "natural religion" Philbert had written about.

Malcolm thought Reginald had figured out a hustle to help him get out of prison. He followed Reginald's instructions and stopped smoking. When pork was served at the prison dining hall, he passed the platter on, telling a fellow inmate that he did not eat pork. News that Malcolm did not eat pork spread among the convicts.

Although he did not know it at the time, Malcolm had taken an important step forward. Long after he had converted to Islam, he looked back on that prison meal and realized that he had submitted to Allah, the Islamic God, for the first time. "I had experienced, for the first time," he wrote in his autobiography, "the Muslim teaching, 'If you will take one step toward Allah—Allah will take two steps toward you.'"[18]

Through the efforts of his half-sister Ella, Malcolm was transferred to the Norfolk Prison Colony, a medium security prison. The prison included an excellent library, which Malcolm used. At first, he read whatever caught his interest, but after the arrival of another letter, both his reading habits and his life changed.

The letter was from his brother Reginald, who said he was coming to visit. Malcolm looked forward to seeing his brother, eager to hear about Reginald's plan for his freedom. Instead of talking about freedom, however, Reginald talked about religion. Reginald explained that Allah had appeared in America before a black man named Elijah Muhammad. Allah had told Elijah that the devil was also a man, and that the devil's time was running out. Reginald then nodded at some white inmates who were talking to their visitors. He told Malcolm that the white man was the devil.

Malcolm recalled the faces and behavior of the white people he had known, beginning from his earliest years in Michigan. He thought about the whites who he believed had broken up his family and sent his mother to an asylum. He thought about the white teacher who had advised him to forego law in favor of carpentry. He remembered shining the shoes of whites at the Roseland, and the white officers who arrested him, and, finally, the white judge who had handed down his stiff prison sentence. What Reginald said made sense, Malcolm concluded. He could certainly agree that many of the whites who had influenced his life had acted as devils.

On his next visit, Reginald told Malcolm about the "true knowledge" of the black man. Malcolm had no identity with his heritage, Reginald said, because the white man had stolen it from him. Reginald explained that in ancient Africa black people had built great civilizations and accumulated vast riches. But evil white men had kidnapped black people, including the Little brothers' ancestors, from their native land and enslaved them in America. By this act of kidnapping, white men had stolen Malcolm's heritage, including land, his true language, and his true name.

Malcolm began to understand that Reginald's way out of prison was not through the prison gate to freedom, but into freedom found in a new state of mind. From daily letters from his brothers and sisters, Malcolm read more of Elijah

Malcolm was transferred to Norfolk Prison in 1947, where he first heard about Elijah Muhammad's teachings.

History "Whitened"

In an interview with Alex Haley published in the June 1963 issue of Playboy, *Malcolm X explained how history had been "whitened." These views were based on Elijah Muhammad's "true knowledge" of the black man, which Malcolm first learned in prison, and on Malcolm's own extensive reading.*

MALCOLM X: "Whole black empires, like the Moorish, have been whitened to hide the fact that a great black empire had conquered a white empire even before America was discovered. The Moorish civilization—black Africans—conquered and ruled Spain; they kept the light burning in Southern Europe. The word "Moor" means "black," by the way. Egyptian civilization is a classic example of how the white man stole great African cultures and makes them appear today as white European. The black nation of Egypt is the only country that has a science named after its culture: Egyptology. The ancient Sumerians, a black-skinned people, occupied the Middle Eastern areas and were contemporary with the Egyptian civilization. The Incas, the Aztecs, the Mayans, all dark-skinned Indian people, had a highly developed culture here in America, in what is now Mexico and northern South America. These people had mastered agriculture at the time when European white people were still living in mud huts and eating weeds. But white children, or black children, or grownups here today in America don't get to read this in the average books they are exposed to.

PLAYBOY: Can you cite any authoritative historical documents for these observations?

MALCOLM X: I can cite a great many, sir. You could start with Herodotus, the Greek historian. He outright described the Egyptians as "black, with woolly hair." And American archaeologist and Egyptologist James Henry Breasted did the same thing.

PLAYBOY: You seem to have based your thesis on the premise that all nonwhite races are necessarily black.

MALCOLM X: Mr. Muhammad says that the red, the brown and the yellow are indeed all part of the black nation. Which means that black, brown, red, yellow, all are brothers, all are one family. The white one is a stranger. He's the odd fellow."

Slavery stripped away the identity of millions of Africans and their descendants in America.

Muhammad's "true knowledge" of the black man. History, he learned, had been "whitened" by white history books. Black people had built great empires in Africa while white people in Europe still lived like animals in caves. But devil white men had perpetuated history's greatest crime, murdering and kidnapping and enslaving millions of black men, women, and children, bringing them to the West in chains.

These acts cut black people off from their origins, eventually producing a "brainwashed" race that was separated from its own language and culture. The white slavemasters began to call their black slaves "Negroes." The whites taught the Negroes to hate their continent of origin, as well as themselves and everything black. The Ne-

groes were taught to worship a white god that looked like the slavemaster.

Although this new true knowledge struck Malcolm "like a blinding light," it was weeks before he could "deal with the direct, personal application to myself, as a black man."[19] As he struggled to accept this new truth, he learned more about Elijah Muhammad, who his siblings called the Messenger of Allah, and the origin of the Nation of Islam in America. He learned that Elijah Muhammad had been born in Georgia, just like their father. During the 1930s, Elijah went to Detroit, where he met Wallace D. Fard, the founder of the Nation of Islam. According to Elijah Muhammad, Wallace D. Fard gave him Allah's message. Fard was God in person, according to Elijah Muhammad.

Turning to Islam

In his biography Malcolm: The Life of a Man Who Changed Black America, *Bruce Perry places Malcolm's conversion to Islam into the context of his life.*

"Two of Malcolm's fellow prisoners sensed that [his sister] Hilda's visit had a decisive impact upon him. At her suggestion, he wrote Elijah Muhammad, the Nation of Islam's leader. Before mailing the letter, he redrafted it about two dozen times.

The reply, which was accompanied by a gift of money, was probably similar to the letters that Elijah sent to scores of other convicts—letters that were apparently designed to alleviate their guilt. The real criminal, Elijah told Malcolm, was not the black lawbreaker but the whites who had allegedly made him turn to crime. It was heady medicine. The Nation of Islam and its austere moral code seemed to offer the respect and acceptance the criminal Malcolm had outwardly scorned but secretly coveted.

So Malcolm turned to religion, as his mother had done during a time of troubles. The leap of faith, which he completed before or by early 1949, was not achieved without conflict; the price was complete submission to Allah. The conflict was so intense that it took Malcolm a week to bend his knees and pray for forgiveness. Every time he began to prostrate himself, something drove him back up. But his need for atonement, he later acknowledged, drove him back down."

Malcolm became more and more interested in Mr. Muhammad and the Nation of Islam. At the suggestion of his sister Hilda, Malcolm wrote to Elijah Muhammad. He received a reply from the "Messenger of Allah" welcoming him into the "true knowledge." The letter enclosed a five-dollar bill.

Malcolm's siblings encouraged him to pray to Allah. Malcolm had found it easy to believe in Elijah Muhammad's version of Islam in his mind, but he found it very difficult to submit and adopt the traditional Muslim posture for prayer. It took him a week to overcome his intense feelings of shame and embarrassment, and remain in the prone position.

Malcolm began to write letters every day. He wrote regular letters to Mr. Muhammad, and to members of his family. He wrote to his hustler friends in the ghetto but received no replies.

Elijah Muhammad greets the cheering crowds at a 1961 Nation of Islam prayer meeting.

Frustrated at not being able to express his inner feelings in his letters, he began to copy pages from a dictionary onto a tablet in an effort to improve his writing skills. Starting with the letter A, he copied one entire page onto his tablet, then moved on to the next page. Eventually he worked his way through the entire dictionary.

He became more serious about his reading, selecting books on history, philosophy, and religion from the prison library. Between his dictionary exercise and his reading, his writing and reading skills improved dramatically.

For the first time in his life, Malcolm actually could understand what he was reading. He spent most of his free time in the prison library, or sitting with a book on his bunk. The books that he read opened up the world outside the confines of his tiny cell, a world that was far removed from the life he had experienced as a street hustler. The time began to pass quickly. "Between Mr. Muhammad's teachings, my correspondence, my visitors—usually Ella and Reginald—and my reading of books, months passed without my even thinking about being imprisoned," he recalled in his autobiography. "In fact, up till then I had never been so truly free in my life."[20]

As his brother Reginald had promised, Malcolm was freeing himself from prison. With the "true knowledge" at hand, Malcolm read widely. He read about ancient civilizations and modern world history. He studied books about the different races and how they had developed. He pored over books about white slave owners and their brutal treatment of black slaves. To Malcolm, Elijah Muhammad's true knowledge of the black man was indeed true. In book after book, Malcolm saw how white men had exploited the world's black, red, yellow, and brown races and made them suffer.

To improve his speaking skills, Malcolm joined the prison colony's weekly debates. He studied each week's topic, then carefully prepared his own arguments. Before the debate, he took the other side, trying to pick his own arguments apart so he could strengthen them.

Malcolm wanted to share the "true knowledge" with the other black convicts. He began to tell them about Elijah Muhammad and the Nation of Islam. He worked slowly, after being warned by his brother Reginald that the black man was at first frightened by the truth.

In March 1950, Malcolm was transferred from Norfolk back to Charlestown Prison. Although Malcolm later blamed the transfer on the prison administration, it is possible that he initiated it himself both to test his new faith in the harsher Charlestown environment and because he had converted all the black prisoners he could reach at Norfolk.

Paroled

In 1952 Malcolm had been in prison for more than six years. Although his sentence was not complete, he could be released from prison on parole if he could find someone to sponsor him. Malcolm's brother Wilfred, who lived in Detroit,

agreed to sponsor Malcolm. In July 1952 Malcolm was paroled.

Instead of returning to his old ghetto haunts in Boston or Harlem, Malcolm went to Detroit, where most of his brothers and sisters lived. He took a job in the same furniture store where Wilfred worked.

For the first time since his conversion to Islam, Malcolm was able to worship in a mosque. He regularly attended Detroit Temple Number One, the first temple established by Elijah Muhammad. Although it was scarcely more than a storefront and its membership was small, Malcolm felt welcome.

Early in September 1952 members of Temple One drove to Chicago to hear Elijah Muhammad speak at Temple Number Two. For the first time, Malcolm saw the man who had saved him while he was in prison.

Malcolm was riveted by the sight of Elijah Muhammad and by the words he spoke. At the end of his sermon, Elijah Muhammad called Malcolm's name and asked him to stand. He praised Malcolm's strength while in prison. He noted that now that he was out of prison, Malcolm could return to his old ways. But, Elijah concluded, he thought Malcolm would remain faithful. Malcolm and his family were invited to join Mr. Muhammad for dinner in his home, and Malcolm was able to speak to the Messenger in person.

He asked Mr. Muhammad how they could increase the membership of the Detroit temple. The Messenger advised Malcolm to recruit new members among the young people. Malcolm determined to follow Mr. Muhammad's advice.

A short time after returning to Detroit, Malcolm made a final important step into

Meeting the Messenger

Malcolm recalled in his Autobiography *the moment in September 1952 when he saw Elijah Muhammad for the first time.*

"I was totally unprepared for the Messenger Elijah Muhammad's physical impact upon my emotions. From the rear of Temple Number Two, he came toward the platform. The small, sensitive, gentle, brown face that I had studied on photographs, until I had dreamed about it, was fixed straight ahead as the Messenger strode, encircled by the marching, strapping Fruit of Islam guards. The Messenger, compared to them, seemed fragile, almost tiny. He and the Fruit of Islam were dressed in dark suits, white shirts, and bow ties. The Messenger wore a gold-embroidered fez.

I stared at the great man who had taken the time to write to me when I was a convict whom he knew nothing about. He was the man whom I had been told had spent years of his life in suffering and sacrifice to lead us, the black people, because he loved us so much. And then, hearing his voice, I sat leaning forward, riveted upon his words."

The Honorable Elijah Muhammad, leader of the Nation of Islam.

the world of Islam. He cast off his last name of "Little" replacing it with the letter "X." Years later, he explained why he had made this change.

> Little is the name of the slavemaster who owned one of my grandparents during slavery, a white man, and the name Little was handed down to my grandfather, to my father, and on to me. But after hearing the teachings of the Honorable Elijah Muhammad and realizing that Little is an English name, and I'm not an Englishman, I gave the Englishman back his name; and since my own had been stripped from me, hidden from me, and I don't know it, I use X; and someday, as we are taught by the Honorable Elijah Muhammad, every black man, woman, and child in America will get back the same name, the same language, and the same culture that he had before he was kidnapped and brought to this country and stripped of these things.[21]

Malcolm had entered Charlestown Prison in 1946 alienated, angry, unskilled, inarticulate, and unfocused. During his years in prison he had educated himself and developed his skills in writing and public speaking. Most significantly of all, he had found Allah in the teachings of Elijah Muhammad and the Nation of Islam.

Now, as Malcolm X, his anger still remained, but for the first time in his life, it was focused beyond himself. He was angry for all black people. He now had a goal—spreading the teachings of Elijah Muhammad. During the next decade, "Malcolm X" would become one of the most controversial and feared names in America.

4 Minister Malcolm X

The first meeting between Malcolm and Elijah Muhammad was the beginning of a new career for Malcolm. It was also the beginning of a deepening connection between Mr. Muhammad and Malcolm, the savior and the saved. During the next decade, Malcolm X and Elijah Muhammad would develop a father-and-son relationship. Malcolm would help build the Nation of Islam into a powerful organization, becoming its national spokesperson.

As he had recruited black convicts while still in prison, Malcolm began to recruit new members for the Nation of Islam's Temple Number One in Detroit. The recruiting process was called "fishing." With other Muslim brothers, Malcolm fished in the ghetto sections of the city, talking to "brainwashed black brothers" in bars, in poolrooms, and on street corners. He was well suited for the job. He had lived the same life as those he approached and could speak to them in a way they understood. He would begin talking to them in street language. When he had captured his listeners' attention, he

Elijah Muhammad and Malcolm X. The two leaders of the Nation of Islam had a father-and-son relationship.

At a 1963 Black Muslim national convention the women, veiled and dressed in white, sit separate from the men.

would talk about the true knowledge and the Nation of Islam.

The fishing was seldom good enough for the ambitious, impatient Malcolm, who soon grew frustrated that so few would make the commitment to join the Nation. But he and his fellow fishermen did not give up. The fishing trips were successful enough that within a few months, the membership of the Detroit temple had tripled.

Malcolm looked forward to the times he was allowed to speak at the temple's regular meetings. He spoke directly to the black faces in the audience, his angry voice rising in contempt as he preached his own version of the "true knowledge of the black man."

He told his audience how white men had dominated black men and kept them begging for crumbs from the table. Often Malcolm turned the white man's historical symbols around and used them to illustrate his own points. Unlike the Pilgrims, Malcolm said, black people did not land on Plymouth Rock in Massachusetts in 1620. Instead, Malcolm told his brothers

and sisters in the audience, Plymouth Rock landed on black people.

Those who stood up at the end of his sermon and became followers of Elijah Muhammad were taught that the "devil white man" was the enemy and should be avoided. They learned that black people should educate themselves. They learned that they should strive to be independent of white people by owning and operating their own businesses. The new members were also taught the strict morality of the Nation of Islam. Muslims could not drink, smoke, or use other drugs. They could not use profanity, or engage in adultery or sex outside of marriage.

Like Father and Son

Malcolm's entire life soon became centered around the Nation of Islam. He left his job to work for the Nation full time. In the summer of 1953, he was made assistant minister of the Detroit temple. On the outside, Malcolm reacted with humility to his new assignment. His humility, however, masked a fierce ambition. He told one of his Muslim brothers that he wanted to become Elijah Muhammad's right-hand man.

Malcolm remained in awe of his kind, almost fatherly leader. He basked in the warmth of Mr. Muhammad's attention, absorbing every word the older man spoke. The Messenger became the loving father figure that Malcolm had imagined his own father to be, and had longed for through his troubled adolescence. In return, Elijah Muhammad often treated Malcolm like a son. Years later, insiders of the Nation of Islam would remark that he treated Malcolm better than his own children.

Malcolm worked hard to learn the organizational and administrative procedures of the Nation. He studied the relationship between the Bible and the Quran, the sacred book of the Muslims. His work was noticed by Elijah Muhammad, who soon sent Malcolm to Boston to organize a new temple there. Malcolm spoke to small groups in the living room of a Muslim brother. In his own words, he told listeners the true knowledge of the black man. Then he asked who was willing to stand up and join the Nation. In three months time, he had recruited enough new members to open a small temple, or mosque.

Malcolm served as the minister of the Boston temple for a short time. In March 1954 he was sent to Philadelphia to form a new mosque there. By May enough members had been recruited to open a temple. From Philadelphia, Malcolm was sent to New York City, where in June he became minister of Temple Number Seven in Harlem.

Malcolm immediately understood the significance of his appointment. He knew that the Nation of Islam needed to grow to help America's millions of black people. More than one million blacks lived in New York City's five boroughs. Malcolm realized that New York offered the best "fishing" potential in America for recruiting new members to the Nation. He was moved by the trust that the Messenger had demonstrated in giving him the assignment.

For the first time since he had fled the streets nine years earlier to escape West Indian Archie, Malcolm returned to Harlem. Looking up old acquaintances, he found that many of them had died or were dying in slow motion, a fate he had escaped by being converted to Islam. West Indian Archie himself was a "ghost" of the person Malcolm remembered. In Archie, who had possessed a remarkable but misused talent with numbers, Malcolm saw the wasted potential of all black people reduced to life on the streets, victims of the white man's society.

Malcolm set about the task of recruiting members to Temple Seven. He and his associates spread leaflets throughout Harlem. They fished in the crowds that had gathered to hear other people speak. They held regular meetings, and at the end of each meeting, Malcolm asked those who were ready to become followers to stand up. Although black people could easily identify with the Nation's message that they were victims of white society, few stood up. Malcolm knew that the Nation of Islam's strict moral code discouraged many people from joining.

In addition to his duties as minister of New York's Temple Seven, Malcolm helped establish temples in Springfield, Massachusetts, and Hartford, Connecticut. In 1955 he traveled to Atlanta to help establish a temple there.

Honoring Elijah Muhammad

In his interview with Alex Haley published in the June 1963 issue of Playboy, *Malcolm X paid tribute to Elijah Muhammad, while at the same time using his own life as an example from which to teach.*

"It was in prison that I first heard the teachings of the Honorable Elijah Muhammad. His teachings were what turned me around. The first time I heard the Honorable Elijah Muhammad's statement, 'The white man is the devil,' it just clicked. I am a good example of why Islam is spreading so rapidly across the land. I was nothing but another convict, a semi-illiterate criminal. Mr. Muhammad's teachings were able to reach into prison, which is the level where people are considered to have fallen as low as they can go. His teachings brought me from behind prison walls and placed me on the podiums of some of the leading colleges and universities in the country. I often think, sir, that in 1946, I was sentenced to eight to ten years in Cambridge, Massachusetts, as a common thief who had never passed the eighth grade. And the next time I went back to Cambridge was in March 1961, as a guest speaker at the Harvard Law School Forum. This is the best example of Mr. Muhammad's ability to take nothing and make something, to take nobody and make somebody."

A member of the Nation of Islam passes out copies of the group's official publication, Muhammad Speaks.

An Incident in Harlem

Although the Nation of Islam was growing faster, now it represented only a tiny fraction of the country's 22 million black people. Malcolm and his associates remained frustrated that they could not recruit more of the 1 million black people living in New York City. On April 14, 1957 an incident occurred in Harlem that shot the Muslims into local prominence. It began when two white policemen, breaking up a scuffle, ordered a number of bystanders to move on. Johnson Hinton and another Muslim brother did not move quickly enough. The police turned on Hinton, who was beaten badly enough to split his scalp open before being hauled away to the precinct house.

The other man called the local Muslim restaurant for help. As the minister of Temple Seven, Malcolm was quickly notified. The temple members began making telephone calls. Within a half-hour, fifty members of the Fruit of Islam, the Nation's security guards, were standing in formation outside the precinct house. Malcolm strode inside and demanded to see Hinton. At first, police denied that he was there. Then they admitted that Hinton was being held but refused to let Malcolm see him. Malcolm declared that until he had seen Hinton and determined that he was being properly cared for, the Muslims outside would not leave.

James Hicks, editor of the weekly Harlem newspaper *Amsterdam News,* who accompanied Malcolm, recalled the moment the men were allowed entry into the precinct house.

We went on in and saw the man, and they had torn his head off—he eventually won $70,000 from the city. One look and [police inspector] McGowen said, "Get him to the hospital." He said, "Mr. X, he's going to be sent to Harlem Hospital—is that all right?" Malcolm said, "That's all we asked." McGowen said, "Would you take the responsibility of sending your people home?" Malcolm said, "I'll do that."

And then, in that dim light, Malcolm stood up and waved his hand, and all those people just disappeared. *Disappeared.* One of the police people said to me, "Did you see what I just saw?" I said, "Yeah." He said, "This is too much power for one man to have." He meant one black man. I'll never forget that.[22]

The episode drew little attention in the daily newspapers, but the news of how the Muslims had successfully confronted the police quickly spread through Harlem. By the next day, everyone was talking about the Muslims with respect and admiration. The police became aware that the Nation of Islam was a new force in the Harlem community.

A Strange Courtship

As a young street hustler, Malcolm had often bragged about his relationships with women. In truth, however, Malcolm found it difficult to trust women. As an adult, he was usually awkward or aloof around women he was interested in. Through the years, Malcolm had been involved in a number of potentially serious relationships that had fallen apart.

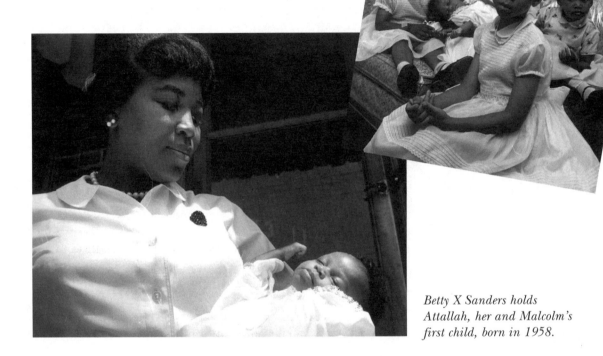

Malcolm's wife and children await his return from Africa in 1964.

Betty X Sanders holds Attallah, her and Malcolm's first child, born in 1958.

In 1956 Malcolm met Betty X Sanders, a nursing student who had recently joined New York's Temple Seven. The two often saw each other at the temple. For about a year Malcolm occasionally found himself thinking about Sister Betty, but rather than trying to get to know her better, he looked for ways to avoid her. In the summer of 1957, Malcolm began to think it was time he got married. He shocked himself by wondering what Betty would answer if he proposed.

He did not find out until the next January, when he proposed in a strange manner. Although he and Betty both lived in New York, Malcolm did not make his proposal in person. Instead, he waited until he had driven from New York to Detroit to visit his brother Wilfred. As soon as he arrived, he impulsively called Betty back in New York and abruptly proposed to her over the telephone. She agreed to marry him, and Malcolm told her to take the next plane to Detroit. When Betty arrived, Malcolm drove them to a city where they could be married immediately. Without fanfare, Malcolm and Betty Sanders were married in a civil ceremony on January 14, 1958. Malcolm admitted years later that he did not really love his wife when they were first married. But as the years passed, he grew to love and trust Betty and their children.

The couple had their first child in November 1958, a daughter they named Attallah. Another daughter, Qubilah, was born in December 1960. The couple's third daughter, Ilyasah, was born in July 1962. A fourth daughter, Gamilah, was born in December 1964. Malcolm did not live to see the twin daughters, Malaak and Malikah, who were born in the fall of 1965 after his death.

A Frightening Message

While the Nation of Islam grew in the black communities of America, the organization remained virtually unknown among white people. That began to change in July 1959, when a five-part television show about the Nation of Islam was broadcast. The series, hosted by journalist Mike Wallace, was entitled "The Hate That Hate Produced." Wallace told viewers that the title reflected "the hatred that a minority of Negroes are returning for the hate the majority of Negroes have received."[23]

Viewers saw frightening images of strong-looking black men engaged in self-defense drills. They saw Muslim women

Members of the Nation of Islam attend a meeting. The movement grew steadily in the late 1950s but was virtually unknown among whites until it was featured in a 1959 television special titled "The Hate That Hate Produced."

Whites verbally abuse black student Elizabeth Eckford in 1957 as she tries to enter previously segregated Little Rock Central High School in Arkansas.

strangely dressed in white scarves and gowns, and black children being taught that the white man was the devil. Viewers heard Malcolm X say that the serpent in the biblical story of Adam and Eve and the Garden of Eden was a symbol for the white man, and that the white man was by nature "evil."

In Malcolm's assessment of the program, what shocked the white viewers was the realization that blacks did not share white people's opinion of themselves. Biographer Bruce Perry described the response to the television broadcast.

> Press reaction was withering. Temple Seven was inundated with angry demands for explanation from news commentators and correspondents from Boston to Tucson. . . . The media spillover caused by the controversial documentary was enormous. Mass cir-

culation weeklies such as *Life, Time,* and *Newsweek* began reporting on the Black Muslim movement. A Harlem radio station invited Malcolm to conduct a weekly talk show. Within four years, three books about the Black Muslims were published.[24]

"The Hate That Hate Produced" and its aftermath firmly established the Nation of Islam as a militant organization that promoted "black racism"—the hatred of whites by black people. The program also helped introduce Malcolm X to the country as the Nation's angry spokesperson.

But the Nation of Islam was doing far more than "teaching hatred." The Nation recruited its members from the criminals, drug addicts, pimps, prostitutes, and hustlers who roamed the streets of America's cities, or were serving time in prison. The Nation's message that they were not criminals, but victims of American society, gave them a new perspective on their lives. From the Nation, converts drew a sense of pride in their skin color.

As it had done for Malcolm X, the Nation of Islam often offered its converts a second chance in life. Through its six-point drug program, addicts were able to get off drugs. The Nation's disciplines helped members find focus and direction in their lives.

Malcolm played a significant role in the Nation's growth. He traveled widely, speaking to audiences in the Nation's temples. He helped to establish new temples in major cities around the country. Through his dedication and effort, the Nation's membership grew. Some sources of the time estimated the Nation's membership at a quarter-million people. Malcolm himself once said the membership grew from about 400 in 1952 to more than 40,000 in ten years. In addition, thousands identified with the Nation and its beliefs but did not become members.

Contrasting Messages

The Great Depression of the 1930s and the focus on World War II until the mid-1940s had retarded the civil rights movements that had sprouted up earlier in the century. The visible, obvious signs of segregation—the separation of blacks and whites—were mostly confined to the South, but black people throughout the nation suffered from discrimination. As America entered a period of growth and prosperity in the 1950s, however, numerous organizations concerned with the condition of black people flourished, and black people again began to speak out, demanding equal rights.

Before the passage of civil rights laws in the 1960s, blacks in the South had to use separate public facilities such as restrooms and water fountains.

In 1955, Rosa Parks (center), shown here on the way to her trial, was arrested for refusing to sit in the colored section of a Montgomery, Alabama, city bus.

This public restroom, like most public places in the South before 1965, is marked for the use of either blacks or whites only.

Groups such as the National Association for the Advancement of Colored People (NAACP), the Student Nonviolent Coordinating Committee (SNCC), and the Southern Christian Leadership Conference (SCLC) all sought to end segregation by working with white people to integrate black people into American society. In an integrated society, blacks and whites would drink from the same fountains, sit at the same lunch counters, and ride buses together. In an integrated society, black people would have the same job opportunities, the same right to vote, the same educational opportunities, and the same respect as white people.

These civil rights groups sought to achieve integration through nonviolent means. If subjected to violence, members of these groups were encouraged to react nonviolently, to "turn the other cheek" as the Bible taught. The integrationist movement had successfully used nonviolent protest to desegregate bus service in Montgomery, Alabama. In 1955 a young black woman, Rosa Parks, refused to give up her seat to a white rider and move to the back of the bus, where black riders were "supposed to" sit. She was arrested. A boycott of the bus company was organized by Dr. Martin Luther King Jr., and other civil rights activists. For 381 days, black people "walked with God" rather than ride the Montgomery buses. The bus company suffered financially and was finally forced to desegregate service in order to survive. Without resorting to violence,

The 1955 boycott of Montgomery city buses by blacks leaves this bus almost empty.

A Vote for Separation

In a debate with integrationist James Farmer entitled "Separation v. Integration," Malcolm X explained the religious origin of the Nation's belief in the separation of blacks from whites. The debate took place at Cornell University in Ithaca, New York, on March 7, 1962, and has been reprinted in numerous texts.

"The Honorable Elijah Muhammad teaches us that the black people in America, the so-called Negroes, are the people who are referred to in the Bible as the lost sheep, who are to be returned to their own in the last days. He says that we are also referred to in the Bible, symbolically, as the lost tribe. He teaches us in our religion that we are those people who the Bible refers to who would be lost until the end of time. . . . And this, basically, is why we who are followers of the Honorable Elijah Muhammad don't accept integration: we feel that we are living at the end of time, by this, we feel that we are living at the end of the world. Not the end of the earth, but the end of the world. . . . We believe that the earth will become all Muslim, all Islam, and because we are in a Christian country we believe that this Christian country will have to accept Allah as God, accept the religion of Islam as God's religion, or otherwise God will come in and wipe it out. And we don't want to be wiped out with the American white man. We don't want to integrate with him, we want to separate from him."

Dr. King and his followers had triumphed. The Montgomery boycott became a symbol of what nonviolent activism could accomplish.

The Nation of Islam stood apart from these organizations in both its beliefs and its methods. The Nation not only rejected segregation, it also rejected integration as a solution to the race issue. Nation members believed in the separation of the races and rejected working with whites. To the Nation's critics, this sounded very similar to the white supremacist rhetoric of groups like the Ku Klux Klan. But Muslims drew a distinction between segregation and separation. Segregation was division of the races forced on black people by white society. Muslims defined separation as a voluntary program by black people who wanted nothing to do with their white enemies. The Nation wanted black people to build their own country within America. For these reasons, the Nation of Islam did not involve itself in the civil rights movement.

The Nation of Islam did not officially advocate violence. Nevertheless, many people feared the opposite because the Nation's militant rhetoric, its rigid discipline, and its self-defense classes gave the organization such a powerful image. Neither did the Nation advocate turning the other cheek, as other black organizations did. The Nation's members were urged to defend themselves if attacked. Because the Nation's members defended themselves,

A New So-Called Negro

During the television program "Where Is the American Negro Headed?" Malcolm X described a "new so-called Negro" that came of age during the civil rights movement of the late 1950s.

"Yes, I think there is a new so-called Negro. We don't recognize the term 'Negro' but I really believe that there's a new so-called Negro here in America. He not only is impatient. Not only is he dissatisfied, not only is he disillusioned, but he's getting very angry. And whereas the so-called Negro in the past was willing to sit around and wait for someone else to change his condition or correct his condition, there's a growing tendency on the part of a vast number of so-called Negroes today to take action themselves, not to sit and wait for someone else to correct the situation. This, in my opinion, is primarily what has produced this new Negro. He is not willing to wait. He thinks that what he wants is right, what he wants is just, and since these things are just and right, it's wrong to sit around and wait for someone else to correct a nasty condition when [someone else gets] ready."

Rev. Dr. Martin Luther King Jr. addresses a civil rights rally. King advocated nonviolent demonstrations for equality.

incidents of violence involving Muslims were not uncommon. Although there is a distinct difference between claiming the right to self-defense and advocating violence, the distinction was often blurred in media coverage. The appearance of Muslim names in newspaper reports only strengthened the growing link in the media between Muslims and violence.

Unlike King, Malcolm X advised blacks to use whatever means necessary to gain equal rights. The media often interpreted this advice as a call for violence.

Malcolm and Martin

As the 1950s ended and the 1960s began, two men symbolized the contrasting ideologies of the Nation of Islam and the integration movement. Although there were many leaders in the integration movement, its champion in those days was Dr. Martin Luther King Jr. Dr. King had been catapulted to prominence by his successful leadership of the Montgomery bus

boycott. Although Elijah Muhammad remained the spiritual leader of the much smaller Nation of Islam, it was Malcolm X who became its national spokesperson. Together, Malcolm and Martin seemed to represent polar opposites in the civil rights movement.

There were similarities and contrasts between the two men. Malcolm was tall and lean, while Martin was shorter and stocky. Malcolm had grown up in poverty, while Martin Luther King had grown up in much better conditions. Both were ministers of their respective faiths. Malcolm, the son of a Baptist minister, had rejected Christianity and was a minister in the Muslim faith. Martin, also the son of a minister, was a Baptist minister himself.

Both men were charismatic, dynamic speakers who could genuinely move their audiences. Their audiences, however, were very different. In his fiery manner, Malcolm spoke directly to impoverished black people. He called himself "the angriest Negro in America." Without fear, he said exactly what many black people felt about white people. He turned the fear blacks had of whites back on whites. He often called on black people to gain their rights as Americans "by any means necessary."

When Dr. King spoke to black people, his message was often directed beyond them toward white people. He sought to educate whites about the experience of America's black people. He knew that

Integration Won't Work

In a television program titled "Where Is the American Negro Headed?" on October 15, 1961, Malcolm X explained why integration would not work.

"It is not a case of integration into the American way of life, nor is it a question of *not* integrating. The question is one of human dignity, and integration is only a method or tactic or role that many of the so-called Negroes are using to get recognition and respect as human beings. And many of these Negroes have gotten lost on the road. They're confusing the objective with the method. Now if integration is the objective, then what will we have after we get integration?

I think that the black man in America wants to be recognized as a human being, and it's almost impossible for one who has enslaved another to bring himself to accept the person who used to pull his plow, who used to be an animal, subhuman, who used to be considered as such by him—it's almost impossible for that person in his right mind to accept that person as his equal."

integration would work only if whites lost their prejudices.

Malcolm was keenly aware that he and King appealed to different audiences. He used this difference to attack King and his nonviolent philosophy in a June 1963 television interview with author Kenneth B. Clark:

> *White* people follow King. *White* people pay King. *White* people subsidize King. *White* people support King. But the masses of black people don't support Martin Luther King, Jr. King is the best weapon that the white man, who wants to brutalize Negroes, has ever gotten in this country, because he is setting up a situation where, when the white man wants to attack Negroes, they can't defend themselves, because King has put this foolish philosophy out— you're not supposed to fight or you're not supposed to defend yourselves.[25]

The differences between the two men and the philosophies their organizations represented were further evident in their roles in the 1963 Civil Rights March on Washington. In August 1963 thousands of people of all races gathered in the nation's capital to march in support of civil rights. During the event, Dr. King stood on the steps of the Lincoln Memorial and delivered one of the most famous civil rights speeches in history. "I have a dream," Dr. King said, "that one day this nation will rise up and live out the true meaning of its creed: We hold these truths to be self-evident, that all men are created equal."[26]

Because of the Nation's policy of nonengagement in the civil rights movement, Malcolm had no role at all in the march. Instead, Malcolm denounced the

In 1963, Dr. King led a civil rights march on Washington, D.C., during which he gave his famous "I Have a Dream" speech. Malcolm X and the Nation of Islam did not take part.

march as a "farce" and a "circus," charging that white people had seized control of the march from the black people who conceived it. White people, Malcolm claimed, had told marchers how and where to arrive, where to assemble, where to march, even what to sing.

He also played off Dr. King's dream imagery in a manner that criticized society and King at the same time. In speeches and appearances he declared that he saw no dream for America's black people, only a nightmare.

Dr. King and other civil rights demonstrators lead the civil rights march on Washington, D.C. in 1963. Malcolm X ridiculed the event as having been taken over by whites.

A Problem for Malcolm

Although Malcolm was devoted to the Nation of Islam and to Elijah Muhammad, he was frustrated with the Messenger's refusal to involve the Nation in the civil rights movement. He knew that among some members of the black community, the Nation of Islam was criticized for talking a lot but not doing much to advance the cause of black people.

Elijah Muhammad had reasons for noninvolvement in addition to those he expressed publicly in his teachings. He feared that political action by him or by the Nation might prompt the U.S. government to act against him. The Nation also enjoyed tax exemptions because it was classified as a religious organization by the federal Internal Revenue Service. Political activity could give government officials an opportunity to argue that the Nation of Islam was not a religious organization and withdraw its tax exemptions.

Despite frustration, Malcolm continued his work. Recognizing his growing popularity and importance, the Messenger had placed great trust in him, giving him a new mission. He had instructed Malcolm to make himself better known around the country. Doing so, Elijah Muhammad believed, also would make himself better known. But the Messenger warned Malcolm that he would encounter jealousy and even hatred from other members of the Nation of Islam.

Malcolm was honored by Elijah Muhammad's faith in him. The directive also fit nicely with his own desire to be more involved in the struggle of all black people. But in becoming better known, Malcolm would draw more attention to himself than to Elijah Muhammad. He had no idea that in fulfilling the Messenger's directive he would ignite jealousy among Elijah Muhammad's other managers. And he had no idea that Elijah would fall victim to his own prophecy.

Chapter

5 A Split with Elijah Muhammad

By the time throngs of civil rights activists had marched in Washington, D.C., singing "We Shall Overcome," Malcolm X was recognized as the most powerful figure in the Nation of Islam, next to the Messenger himself. But throughout the early 1960s, as Malcolm helped build the Nation, he had ambitions to do even more for the cause of black America. He began to take his militant message beyond the Nation of Islam to a wider audience. His ambition, combined with a scandal within the Nation of Islam, produced a chain of events that would force him to break with Elijah Muhammad and the Nation.

Malcolm toured the country, speaking at the Nation's gatherings, and increasingly addressing white America through radio and television. He became a familiar, angry face in the media. Despite his militancy, or perhaps because of it, he became the second most popular speaker on

Malcolm X, speaking at one of the Nation's temples, thanks his audience for their generous contribution to the cause.

James Meredith was the first black student at the University of Mississippi. Although the government forced the university to accept Meredith, Malcolm X called the event mere tokenism.

the college circuit. Ironically, the most popular speaker was Barry Goldwater, the conservative Republican senator from Arizona.

The press began to pay attention to Malcolm's frank, unyielding evaluation of the black man's place in white society. Much of his criticism was directed at the achievements of the civil rights movement. He criticized the very concept of integration as being insufficient. To Malcolm, being allowed to sit down at a lunch counter with white people or ride next to whites on a bus did not make up for more than 300 years of discrimination. When National Guard troops were sent to the all-white University of Mississippi so that James Meredith, a black student, could safely attend classes, Malcolm did not compliment U.S. Marshals who had escorted Meredith to

class and forced the university to accept him as a student. Instead he labeled the event an example of "token integration."

White people who worked for civil rights got no word of thanks from Malcolm. He called liberal northern whites who participated in southern civil rights demonstrations as "hypocrites" because they did nothing about racial problems in their own communities. With a biting wit that carried the true meaning of his words, he "complimented" southern whites in his autobiography for being "honest."

> [The Southern white man] bares his teeth to the black man; he tells the black man to his face that Southern whites will never accept phony "integration." The Southern white goes further, to tell the black man that he means to fight him every inch of the way—against the so-called "tokenism." The advantage of this is the Southern black man never has been under any illusions about the opposition he is dealing with.[27]

Malcolm also continued to rebuke black leaders of the civil rights movement for working with white people to achieve their goals. In his criticism, he often drew on old slavery terms. He pointed out that white slave owners used to handpick some slaves to serve in the yard or house. These "house Negroes" were treated much better than the "field Negroes" who worked in the cotton fields. To maintain their privileged status, house Negroes began to identify with and support their master, Malcolm said. Malcolm dismissed modern black leaders as house Negroes, handpicked by whites to play token roles to the civil rights struggle. These black leaders, Malcolm insisted, were as much interested in maintaining their own status as they were in helping all black people. He insulted black leaders by calling them "Uncle Toms." His attacks spared no one, not even Dr. King, the most respected civil rights leader in the country.

Malcolm's statements disturbed almost everyone, but few were more disturbed than the Messenger himself. In his view, Malcolm was breaking the policy of nonengagement in the civil rights movement. Intellectually, Malcolm had grown during the ten years since he had first fished for recruits in the Detroit ghettos. Increasingly, he had begun to do his own thinking. He secretly harbored doubts about the true knowledge of the black man and other teachings of the Messenger. He disagreed with Elijah Muhammad's official policy of nonengagement in the civil rights struggle. To Malcolm, the Nation could be a more significant force in the struggle of American blacks if its members took more action. Wherever black people stood up against racism, Malcolm believed that militant members of the Nation of Islam should be present. Malcolm feared that if the Muslims did not become more active in seeking civil rights, the masses of black people would stop taking the Nation seriously.

Servant or Rival?

Malcolm's frustration over nonengagement was not the only conflict he had with the Messenger and other officials in the Nation of Islam. By Elijah Muhammad's command, Malcolm had become the second most powerful individual in the Nation. In making this decision, Mr.

Muhammad had passed over some of his own children. As a result, some of the younger Muhammads and their associates became jealous of Malcolm, just as the Messenger had predicted.

For a couple of years, Malcolm had heard remarks concerning his role in the Nation. At different times he heard that he was "trying to take over the Nation of Islam" and that he was "taking credit" for the Messenger's teachings. At other times, he learned that some were accusing him of trying to "build an empire" within the Nation of Islam and making a "pile of money." In truth Malcolm had nothing more than his automobile and the seven-room house he lived in with his wife Betty and their children. The Nation had given

Malcolm at a Nation rally. After Elijah Muhammad himself, Malcolm was the most well-known speaker outside the Nation of Islam.

Malcolm the house. He had even left the title of the house in the Nation's name, a decision he would later regret.

Elijah Muhammad's family, however, had become quite wealthy through its control of the Nation's extensive financial empire. Through the years, the family's finances had become so intertwined with the Nation's that it was difficult to tell what belonged to whom. Later investigations would determine that the Muhammad family had in fact diverted for personal use funds collected from the Nation's membership.

The Muhammad family feared that Malcolm was trying to take control of the Nation. If Malcolm had real ambitions about taking over the Nation, he was successful in keeping them hidden. With rumors of jealousy flying all around him, he tried to stand outside the spotlight while doing his job. He always began his public statements with "The Honorable Elijah Muhammad says, . . . " to give full credit to the Messenger. When members of the press asked for his photograph, he instead handed out pictures of Elijah Muhammad. He began refusing interviews, so the others could not claim he was trying to capture the limelight. It bothered him to turn down offers, because he viewed each refusal as a lost opportunity to advance the position of black people.

Malcolm began to notice signs that he was falling out of favor with other members of the Nation. As early as 1962, he realized that he was receiving less and less coverage in *Muhammad Speaks*, a newspaper he had founded a few years earlier. He learned that Mr. Muhammad's son Herbert, the paper's publisher, had instructed that "as little as possible be printed" about him. Soon his name was no longer mentioned in the paper at all.

Betrayed

Malcolm realized that his attempts to neutralize the jealousy of other Nation officials were preventing him from speaking out on the key events of the day. Still, he coped with the situation as best he could and continued to do his job. The Messenger, after all, had warned him about jealousy. But he was unable to cope with persistent rumors that the Messenger himself was acting immorally.

When Malcolm became a Muslim in his prison cell, he renounced his old habits of substance abuse and immoral sexual behavior. Avoiding vices and immoral sexual behavior was at the very core of being a Muslim. Those guilty of the im-

Elijah Muhammad, known to his followers as the Messenger of Allah, had been having affairs with female members of his staff. When Malcolm found out, he became greatly disillusioned.

A Total Fool

Malcolm explained in his Autobiography *that keeping the secret about Elijah Muhammad made him feel like "a total fool."*

"There was never any specific moment when I admitted the situation to myself. In the way that the human mind can do, somehow I slid over admitting to myself the ugly fact, even as I began dealing with it.

Both in New York and Chicago, non-Muslims whom I knew began to tell me indirectly they had heard—or they would ask me if I had heard. I would act as if I had no idea whatever of what they were talking about—and I was grateful when they chose not to spell out what they knew. I went around knowing that I looked to them like a total fool. I felt like a total fool, out there every day preaching, and apparently not knowing what was going on right under my nose, in my own organization, involving the very man I was praising so. To look like a fool unearthed emotions I hadn't felt since my Harlem hustler days. The worse thing in the hustler's world was to be a dupe."

moral practices of adultery or fornication were disciplined by isolation or expulsion from the Nation by the Messenger himself. The guilty were to be shunned by other Muslims. For years, Malcolm had shunned his own brother, Reginald, who had been isolated from the Nation for immoral behavior.

As early as 1955, Malcolm had heard rumors about the Messenger. At first, he dismissed them because "for me even to consider believing anything as insane-sounding as any slightest implication of any immoral behavior of Mr. Muhammad—why the very idea made me shake with fear."[28] The idea upset Malcolm for several reasons. He hated to accept the possibility that the man he believed had raised him from the dead was immoral. Undoubtedly, too, he understood that if such rumors were confirmed and became public, irreparable harm would be done to the Nation's reputation, and its members would feel betrayed.

Finally, the rumors became so persistent that Malcolm could no longer ignore them. He conducted his own investigation and confirmed that at least two of the Messenger's secretaries had become pregnant and were quietly isolated from the Nation. He also learned that the Messenger considered him, Malcolm, dangerous and that Elijah Muhammad had fallen victim to his own prophecy about jealousy and hatred. While praising Malcolm in public, privately the Messenger was being very critical of his protégé. When Malcolm learned this, he felt foolish for having praised Elijah Muhammad while the Messenger had been criticizing him behind his back.

In April 1963, Malcolm and Mr. Muhammad met in Phoenix, Arizona, where the Messenger lived because of his frail health. Malcolm told the Messenger about what he had learned. In answer to Malcolm's questions, Elijah Muhammad compared himself to the biblical figure David, who had taken more than one wife. He told Malcolm that he was fulfilling prophecy.

Now Malcolm felt more than foolish. Elijah Muhammad was the source that all Nation members turned to for inspiration in their resistance to immoral temptation. Malcolm felt that Elijah Muhammad had betrayed not only him, but the Muslim faith and all his followers with his immoral behavior.

The events that followed this conversation were interpreted as evidence of a plot by each man, Elijah Muhammad and Malcolm, against the other. Both men harbored many feelings that contributed to the acrimony that developed between them. For Malcolm, his life was the Nation of Islam. Through the teachings of Elijah Muhammad, he had been saved. But as a spokesperson for black people, Malcolm was outgrowing the Nation. He disagreed with Mr. Muhammad's decision to remain aloof from the civil rights struggle. He also felt betrayed by the Messenger's immorality. If Malcolm left the Nation, however, he would be leaving behind his support, or power base.

In turn, the Messenger felt betrayed by Malcolm. He was angered by the independence Malcolm showed. He interpreted Malcolm's discussion of the scandal with others as a plot against himself. The Nation of Islam was also his life, and he sought to protect himself and the Nation's holdings.

Shortly after his conversation with the Messenger, Malcolm was transferred from New York to the temple in Washington, D.C. The transfer was called a promotion, but Malcolm saw it as an attempt to wrest control of the New York mosque away from him. There was more at stake than the spiritual care of the Nation's New York members. The New York mosque contributed a great deal of money to the Nation's treasury. Whoever controlled New York controlled that money. By transferring Malcolm to Washington, officials in Chicago, which was the Nation's headquarters, hoped to gain control of New York, and cut Malcolm off from his support there.

But Malcolm counteracted the transfer by shuttling back and forth between his new assignment in Washington and his old temple in New York. In a move that defied Elijah Muhammad's nonengagement policy, Malcolm directly involved the Nation in the civil rights movement by announcing that the New York temple would conduct a voter registration drive. Later, Malcolm publicly advocated a united front between the Nation and other black organizations, another departure from the nonengagement policy.

These actions antagonized the Messenger and his supporters. Not only was Malcolm counteracting their effort to end his control of the New York temple, he was also showing more and more independence.

Some time during these weeks, Malcolm told six other Muslim officials on the East Coast about Mr. Muhammad's immorality. Some of them already knew. In his *Autobiography,* Malcolm justified his actions on the grounds of preparing the Muslim officials to teach that Elijah Muhammad's immorality was merely the fulfillment of prophecy, as the two men had discussed during their meeting in the Messenger's home in Phoenix. Word of Malcolm's candid conversation with these officials quickly traveled back to the Chicago temple. The Chicago officials interpreted Malcolm's act as a plot against the Messenger. A bitter behind-the-scenes struggle broke out between Malcolm and the Chicago Muslims. In his *Autobiography,* Malcolm claimed to have been caught by surprise by the events that unfolded during the remainder of the year. In his view, he was only trying to prepare

his fellow ministers to handle the scandal once it became public.

In August 1963, Malcolm was removed as minister of Washington's Temple Four. Publicly, both Malcolm and the Nation of Islam took pains not to advertise this change as a demotion. The Nation simply stated that a permanent replacement minister had been found. Malcolm told *Jet* magazine that the job was "just too much for him." Those who knew Malcolm well, however, knew also that he had been supervising all the East Coast mosques for years.

In public, Malcolm continued to speak his mind, straying far beyond Mr. Muhammad's policy of nonengagement. In one speech, he seemed to favor the idea of a black political party. In another speech, without specifically saying so, he gave the impression that he advocated

"We Are Going to Get Rid of Him"

In "Malcolm X as a Husband and Father," Betty X Shabazz suggests a motive for Malcolm's suspension from the Nation of Islam late in 1963. The essay appears in Malcolm X: The Man and His Times, *edited by John Henrik Clarke.*

"As far as Malcolm's suspension from the movement was concerned, if it hadn't happened because of the remarks he is supposed to have made about John Kennedy, it would have occurred for some other reason. Malcolm was told two years before this happened that [officials] were trying to get rid of him. At that time he was also told several other things they were planning to do. Certain people in the movement felt that he had gotten too big, that he was trying to get a power base for himself. One of Malcolm's supporters said to the officials, 'How can you say this when everything the man does is for the Nation?' They said, 'Well, regardless of what he does or who he does it for, we are going to get rid of him whenever we can.'"

revolution, a position frowned on by Elijah Muhammad.

Silenced

Malcolm's actions continued to infuriate Elijah Muhammad and his associates. They needed a way to silence him. The opportunity came in the form of a national tragedy. On November 22, 1963, President John F. Kennedy was assassinated in Dallas, Texas. Three days later, filling in for the ailing Elijah Muhammad, Malcolm spoke on "God's Judgment of White America." In a question-and-answer session following his speech, he described Kennedy's death in terms of "chickens coming home to roost." The white man's hate had not stopped with killing black people, Malcolm said, but had kept spreading and claimed the nation's president.

The ill-timed remark was widely publicized and struck a raw nerve in a shocked and grieving nation. The following day, in their regular monthly meeting, the Messenger told Malcolm that the remark could make it hard on Muslims in general. He instructed Malcolm that he not speak in public for ninety days. This "silencing," the Messenger said, would disassociate the Nation from Malcolm's "blunder."

When Malcolm returned to New York, he found that the Chicago officials had already notified the New York temple of the discipline. The New York newspapers had also been notified. Malcolm had never seen the Chicago officials initiate such a quick and thorough public relations campaign.

President John F. Kennedy. Malcolm X was widely criticized for saying that Kennedy's assassination was an example of the hatred typical of whites.

A Difficult Decision

Bruce Perry offers perspective on the decision Malcolm faced regarding his future with the Nation of Islam in Malcolm: The Life of a Man Who Changed Black America.

"Difficult as it may have been for Malcolm to stay in the Nation of Islam, it was apparently just as difficult for him to leave the movement, whose by-laws prohibited believers from terminating their membership voluntarily. (Except for dismissal, the by-laws listed death as the only permissible avenue of departure.) How could he repudiate the very man who had raised him up[?] . . .

If Malcolm left the Nation, where was he to go? The movement was his sole source of financial and organizational support. According to [author Louis] Lomax, Malcolm was hoping to wait things out until he could take over and "purify" the [Nation], which he bitterly declared had been ruined by "niggers." But it was becoming increasingly evident that neither Elijah Muhammad nor anyone else in Chicago would ever allow Malcolm to succeed the Messenger. In short, Malcolm was in conflict. He did not appear able to leave the Nation. Yet, in the long run, he couldn't stay. He couldn't overtly rebel without losing his only secure political base—and perhaps his life. Yet how could he submit much longer?"

Malcolm decides to leave the Nation of Islam.

Death Threat

Malcolm soon found that he had been silenced in the classroom as well and could no longer teach at New York's Temple Seven. Later, he heard that he would be reinstated in ninety days if he submitted to Mr. Muhammad's discipline. Malcolm believed that he already had submitted. After Malcolm's death, his widow recalled how difficult the suspension had been for her husband:

> The time of his suspension was one of confusion and reassessment. At that time, he still had that faith and trust in Elijah Muhammad and was still willing to do his bidding. At one point during those ninety days he was sent a letter asking him to do certain things. He carried out the instructions and was then reprimanded for doing what he had been instructed to do. I think this was the breaking point.[29]

For the first time, according to his *Autobiography*, he began to grow suspicious. But there was more to come. Shortly thereafter, word reached Malcolm that one of his own assistants was secretly criticizing his discussion of the scandal with other ministers. The assistant claimed that members of Harlem's Temple Seven would kill Malcolm if they knew what he had done behind the Messenger's back.

Malcolm interpreted his assistant's remarks as a veiled death threat. He believed that any talk involving references to killing within the Nation of Islam could be initiated only by the Messenger himself. Malcolm decided that he was being set up to be killed.

Malcolm's suspicion that his life was in danger was soon confirmed. Another assistant at the Harlem mosque came to him and confessed that he, the Muslim brother, had been ordered to kill Malcolm. After this incident, Malcolm began to separate himself emotionally from the Nation of Islam.

As the year 1964 began, Malcolm wrestled with his future. He understood that deciding to leave the Nation of Islam—which looked like the most difficult decision of his life—was really no decision at all. The events that had unfolded since his conversation with the Messenger in April 1963 had destroyed his future with the Nation of Islam. He believed that his life was in danger. Still, he found it very difficult to think of life outside of the Nation.

> I was racking my brain. What was I going to do? My life was inseparably committed to the American black man's struggle. I was generally regarded as a "leader." For years, I had attacked so many so-called "black leaders" for their shortcomings. Now, I had to honestly ask myself what I could offer, how I was genuinely qualified to help the black people win their struggle for human rights.[30]

Malcolm considered his options. He was well known in New York. He had an international reputation. He felt he had a message for blacks and that they would listen.

The March 8, 1964, edition of the *New York Times* carried the announcement that Malcolm X was ending his ties with the Nation of Islam. He was starting a new organization of his own.

Chapter

6 His Own Man

Malcolm's painful but necessary split from the Nation of Islam opened the door to a new, uncertain future. For many reasons, the decision would become the most important choice of his life. Leaving the Nation freed Malcolm from Mr. Muhammad's policy of nonengagement in the civil rights movement. Malcolm, for the first time in his life, could speak his mind fully on any issue. He was free to commit his energy to

Malcolm X makes his first public appearance after breaking away from the Nation of Islam. Without the Nation's resources, his audience remained small.

any activity he believed would advance the condition of black people.

But there were problems as well as new freedoms. At the Nation of Islam, Malcolm had the admiration and support of many fellow Muslims. He had access to the Nation's finances to pay his travel and organizational expenses. Now, he had only a handful of followers. He had no money. Even his house was officially owned by the Nation of Islam, which immediately notified Malcolm that he, his wife, and their four children had to move out.

A New Organization

While Malcolm debated the advantages and disadvantages of his decision to leave the Nation, he also evaluated the position of America's 22 million black people. He observed in his autobiography that black people were sick in a number of ways. They were mentally sick, because they accepted domination by white society. Because black people also accepted the white man's version of Christianity, they were also spiritually sick. He believed that blacks were economically sick because as consumers they were content with less than their share of America's wealth. As producers, blacks put little back into the economy. Finally, Malcolm believed black people were politically sick because they did not band together in a bloc and use their votes to get what they wanted.

Malcolm knew he wanted to address these problems. He felt that he could do so by creating a new organization.

In public Malcolm downplayed the split between himself and the Messenger as he outlined the goals of his new organization, which he named the Muslim Mosque, Incorporated. On March 20, 1964, just twelve days after formally announcing his split, he was interviewed on Philadelphia radio station WDAS by Joe Rainey. He acknowledged "opposition within the movement" but insisted that "I love the Honorable Elijah Muhammad and what he is teaching."[31] The purpose of the Muslim Mosque, Inc., Malcolm told the radio audience,

> will be to launch an action program in the community to show our people how to solve our own problems right now. It's true we are going somewhere: we're all going back home [to Africa]. But before we go back home we still have to eat, we still have to sleep, and we still have to have clothes and jobs and education. So we are evolving an action program that will enable us to take the techniques of the Honorable Elijah Muhammad and carry [them] into practice right now in the so-called Negro community and eliminate some of the ills, the social ills and political ills and the economic ills, that keep our people imprisoned and trapped there in the ghetto.[32]

Although Malcolm claimed to have no differences with the Messenger and denied that he was trying to lure members away from the Nation of Islam, he in fact was. But for numerous reasons, Malcolm's efforts were unsuccessful and the organization remained small. First, the Nation conducted an extensive internal campaign to discredit Malcolm and turn him into an enemy. He was denounced in *Muhammad Speaks,* the nation's newspaper. Malcolm found it difficult to woo Nation members as he struggled to build a new power base.

Money was another problem. It was difficult to make the organization grow without money to spend on recruitment and other expenses, and Malcolm had no funds of his own. To raise money, he traveled almost constantly. His long absences made him unavailable to attend to day-to-day operation of the Mosque, as he had done at the Nation. Although Malcolm had frequently delegated tasks to others within the Nation of Islam, he was unable to trust his associates to assume responsibility at the Muslim Mosque, Inc., for similar jobs.

Militant or Moderate?

If Malcolm did not have an identity problem in his own mind, he at least had an image problem. His image problem was connected to those from whom he wanted to draw his political and financial support. It took money to do the things Malcolm wanted to do. To get people to give him money, Malcolm had to appear to represent their ideals. During his years with the Nation of Islam, Malcolm had developed a following of militant blacks who supported separatism and the establishment of a black nation within America. He wanted to keep their support.

The Reverend Milton Galamison (left) leads a desegregation demonstration at a New York City school. Malcolm wanted to take part but feared losing support from militant black separatists.

At the same time, Malcolm sought to broaden his support to include the black people who favored more moderate programs to end racial problems in America.

Malcolm's desire to appeal to both militants and moderates created a dilemma. How could he shift his position without losing his credibility in both groups? The dilemma was demonstrated when the Reverend Milton Galamison organized a civil rights demonstration to end what amounted to segregation in New York City's public schools. Malcolm could not march in the demonstration without appearing to favor integration. On the other hand, if he did not march, he would lose an opportunity to gain support from more moderate blacks.

Faced with such dilemmas at every turn, Malcolm tried to solve them by appearing to be both moderate and militant at the same time. In one of his most famous speeches, for example, he talked about using "ballots" and "bullets" in the same sentence. "Well if you and I don't use the ballot," Malcolm said, "we're going to be forced to use the bullet."[33] Both militants and moderates heard what they wanted to hear. Moderates reacted positively to his call to use the ballot to achieve his goals. Militants, on the other hand, were free to interpret the reference to using bullets as a veiled endorsement of violence.

Pilgrimage to Mecca

Shortly after the formation of the Muslim Mosque, Inc., Malcolm decided to embark on a trip to Mecca, the holy city of Islam. He had both spiritual and political reasons for making this trip. Muslims from all over the world try to make at least one pilgrimage, or hajj, to the holy city. Thus by going to Mecca, Malcolm would be fulfilling his duty to God as a Muslim.

Malcolm was also looking for a truer version of Islam. For years he had understood that Mr. Muhammad had molded Islam to serve his own beliefs. Often Malcolm had defended the Nation of Islam against public criticisms such as a *Newsweek* article published in 1962 that noted "the Messenger calls the message Islam, to the embarrassment of orthodox Muslims in the U.S."[34] Malcolm himself was sometimes approached informally after his speaking engagements by people with white complexions who told him that he was not practicing true Islam.

There were political reasons behind Malcolm's planned hajj, as well. To go forward on his own, Malcolm needed to publicly disassociate himself from Elijah Muhammad and the Nation of Islam. He also needed to shed his old image. Among blacks and whites alike, he was strongly associated with the Nation's teachings that the white man was the devil. By going to Mecca, Malcolm could both experience spiritual renewal and make a clean political break from his old roots.

Malcolm left the United States on April 13. He flew first to Frankfurt, Ger-

Throngs of Muslim pilgrims circle the Ka'aba within the courts of Mecca's Great Mosque. Malcolm X's pilgrimage here changed his attitude about relations between whites and blacks.

many, then to Cairo, Egypt, where he spent two days as a tourist. From Cairo, he flew on to Jedda, Saudi Arabia. In Jedda, Malcolm's hajj was stalled. Only true Muslims may enter the holy city of Mecca. Malcolm first needed to appear before the Hajj Committee Court, which would interview him and rule whether he was a true Muslim. During this one-day wait to appear before the court, Malcolm was treated courteously and helped by people he would have considered white in America. Malcolm found their willingness to help him, a black man, remarkable.

He later recalled that during his waiting period, he began to reassess his old views about the so-called "white man." He realized that in America, the term "white man" meant something more than an individual with white skin. The term also described the individual's attitudes and actions directed toward black people and other non-white races. In America, Malcolm had found those attitudes and actions to be negative.

> But in the Muslim world, I had seen that men with white complexions were more genuinely brotherly than anyone else had ever been.
>
> That morning was the start of a radical alteration in my whole outlook about "white men." [35]

It also marked the beginning of his political separation from Elijah Muhammad and the Nation of Islam.

The next day, Malcolm appeared before the Hajj Committee Court. After questioning Malcolm to determine his sincerity, the judge ruled that Malcolm could proceed to Mecca.

Once in the holy city of Mecca, Malcolm followed the ancient Muslim rituals. He removed his sandals and entered the

Malcolm worships in a mosque in Cairo while on his way to Mecca. He was amazed at how well he was treated by the whites he met in other countries.

Great Mosque. Thousands of Muslims were moving in a circle around Ka'aba, the shrine in which is embedded the sacred Black Stone of Islam. Muslim tradition holds that ancient leaders had circled the Ka'aba. In a similar manner, Malcolm circled the Ka'aba seven times in a counter-clockwise direction. On the seventh circle, he prostrated himself, his head on the floor, and said special prayers. Next he drank water from the holy well of Zem Zem.

Three separate times that day, he made his seven circles around the Ka'aba. The next day, in the company of thousands, he set out at sunrise for Mount Arafat. The group arrived about noon and prayed and chanted until sunset. Standing on Mount Arafat, Malcolm had completed his pilgrimage. He cast the traditional seven stones at the devil, to show that he stood opposed to the forces of evil.

In performing these ancient rituals, Malcolm had fulfilled his duty to Allah. He wrote long letters to his wife explaining his experiences and his new understanding about white people.

> There were tens of thousands of pilgrims, from all over the world. They were of all colors, from blue-eyed blonds to black-skinned Africans. But we were all participating in the same ritual, displaying a spirit of unity and brotherhood that my experiences in America had led me to believe never could exist between the white and the non-white.[36]

He wrote similar letters to associates at the Muslim Mosque, Inc., which he instructed to be copied and distributed to the press. Malcolm signed these letters with a new Islamic name that symbolized his embrace of the true Islam. He signed his letters El-Hajj Malik El-Shabazz.

Malcolm did not return immediately to Harlem after his hajj. Instead he traveled around the Middle East and Africa. In Saudi Arabia, he met with Prince Faisal, the nation's ruler, who had made him a guest of the state. Like other orthodox Muslims in the Middle East, the prince had followed news reports about the Black Muslims. In their meeting Prince Faisal told Malcolm that the Black Muslims were not practicing a true form of Islam. The prince's remark, of course, helped Malcolm to distance himself from the Black Muslims.

Malcolm flew to Beirut, Lebanon, then back to Cairo. From there, he journeyed to Lagos, Nigeria, where he spoke at Ibadan University and made appearances on radio and television. In Accra, Ghana, he was received by a small colony of "Afro-Americans" living there, who had formed a Malcolm X committee to greet him. He met with government officials. He stopped briefly at the airport in Dakar, Senegal, where he shook hands and signed autographs. He arrived in another African capital, Algiers, on May 19, 1964, his thirty-ninth birthday.

Malcolm finally began the long flight back to the United States. He considered the significance of his trip. He had completed his hajj to the holy city of Mecca. He had been received graciously by heads of state and celebrated by brother Muslims. He had spoken about the black man's situation in America. He now realized that he was well known throughout the Muslim world. He felt that Muslims and Africans were keenly aware of racial problems in the United States.

On May 21, Malcolm landed in New York. He talked briefly with the fifty or sixty reporters who were awaiting him, along with his wife and children. Later that day, he held a press conference in Harlem.

As he recalled in his *Autobiography*, Malcolm used the Harlem press conference to tell reporters and the nation that his discovery of the "true Islam" during his hajj had broadened his perspective. He now recognized that there were sincere white people. Although he had dismissed all whites as devils in the past, he would never again be guilty of making such sweeping racist statements.

But at the same time, Malcolm sprang a surprise on the reporters, one that clouded his new image. He announced that he had gathered support among new nations in Africa to bring the United States before the United Nations on charges of discrimina-

A smiling Malcolm X arrives back in the United States a changed man after his tour of the Middle East.

Hidden Motives

Bruce Perry suggests in Malcolm: The Life of a Man Who Changed Black America, *that Malcolm's attempt to internationalize the struggle of black people was aimed at gaining the financial and political support denied him at home.*

"But seeking votes from friendly governments was not the only reason Malcolm returned to Africa seven weeks after he left it. His highly publicized attempt to internationalize Black America's struggle for equal opportunity afforded a perfect cover for his unpublicized attempts to obtain abroad the financial support that was foreclosed to him at home. . . .

Malcolm's return to Africa was also an attempt to secure abroad the political support he lacked at home, where church-based groups like the Southern Christian Leadership Conference wouldn't have anything to do with him. Neither would 'respectable' middle-class organizations like the NAACP and the Urban League. Malcolm was paying the price for his polemical attacks; he had alienated the only American organizations with which he had interests in common. He publicly acknowledged the problem:

'You can't build a power base here. . . . No, you have to have that somewhere else. You can work here, but you'd better put your base somewhere else.'"

tion against American blacks. Malcolm's surprise announcement, rather than his broadened perspective, was the focus of the opening paragraphs of a story in the next day's *New York Times.*

Malcolm X, the Negro nationalist leader, said yesterday he had received pledges of support from some new African nations for charges of discrimination against the United States in the United Nations.

The case against the United States for its treatment of the Negro people, he said, would be prepared and submitted to the United Nations sometime this year. He did not say which nations intended to lodge the formal charges.[37]

The slant of the story in the *New York Times* indicated that Malcolm's hajj had accomplished only part of his goals. It had been an epic physical and spiritual journey. Malcolm had traveled thousands of miles through the Middle East and Africa and had made important political contacts. He had renewed himself spiritually and identified himself with orthodox Islam.

Malcolm had taken these steps to separate himself politically from his old image. But as the *Times* story indicated, many missed his new perspective and continued to view Malcolm as an extremist. For the rest of his life, Malcolm would have to tell America over and over again that he had changed.

From Nationalism to Internationalism

If Malcolm's pilgrimage to Mecca gave him an opportunity to distance himself from the Nation of Islam, it also broadened his thinking. His tour of Africa solidified his belief that black people in Africa and America were struggling against the same problem—the white man's domination.

In the United States, blacks had been enslaved for two centuries before the Civil War ended slavery. But neither the Civil War nor constitutional amendments nor court decisions had really ended the white man's domination over black people. Black people were still suppressed. White European nations had carved Africa into colonies and stripped the land of its riches. Black people were struggling to break the bonds of colonialism and reestablish self-rule over their own lands.

Malcolm believed that the black people of both continents could unite and work together to fight their common enemy. By the time he returned to New York, Malcolm had already conceived of a bold plan to build unity between African and American blacks. He intended to use this unity to bring the question of American racism before the United Nations.

Although the reporters to whom Malcolm introduced this plan at the press conference after his return to New York quickly dropped the subject, Malcolm did not. In June 1964, he established the Organization of Afro-American Unity (OAAU). The OAAU was patterned after the Organization of African Unity (OAU), established in Ethiopia in 1963 to promote solidarity among African nations. The preamble of its charter stated that the OAAU was:

> DETERMINED to unify the Americans of African descent in their fight for Human Rights and Dignity, and being fully aware that this is not possible in the present atmosphere and condition of oppression, we dedicate our selves to the building of a political, economic, and social system of justice and peace;

> DEDICATED to the unification of all people of African descent in this hemisphere and to the utilization of that unity to bring into being the organizational structure that will project the black people's contributions to the world . . .

> DESIROUS that all Afro-American people and organizations should henceforth unite so that the welfare and well-being of our people will be assured. . . .[38]

In July 1964, the Organization of African Unity held a summit conference, which Malcolm attended. Although he was not allowed to address the conference, he did present a memorandum that linked the racial problems of the two continents. The OAU passed a resolution that applauded the passage of the U.S. Civil Rights

Defining Himself

Malcolm's continuing need to distance himself from Elijah Muhammad, and his attempts to appeal to both militants and moderates are evident in this exchange during an interview with television personality Les Crane, on December 2, 1964. The interview is published in Malcolm X: The Last Speeches, *edited by Bruce Perry.*

"*Crane:* Integration offends you. You don't believe in the use of that word. You prefer to think of it as brotherhood which is, for the purposes of our discussion, going to be the same thing. But in the old days you didn't believe in brotherhood, you believed in pure strict separation, didn't you?

Malcolm X: Whenever I opened my mouth, I always said that Elijah Muha—the Honorable Elijah Muhammad— teaches us thus and so. And I spoke for him. I represented him. I represented an organization and organizational thinking. Many of my own views that I had from personal experience I kept to myself. I was faithful to that organization and to that man. Since things came about that made me doubt his integrity, I thought—I think for myself, I listen as much as I can to everyone and try to come up with a capsule opinion, capsulized opinion. I believe that it is possible for brotherhood to be brought about among all people, but I don't delude myself into dreaming or falling for a dream that this exists before it exists. Some of the American—some of the leaders of our people in this country always say that they, you know, they believe in this dream. But while they're dreaming, our people are having a nightmare, and I don't think that you can make a dream come true by pretending that that dream exists when it doesn't."

After his break with the Nation of Islam, Malcolm began to speak for himself rather than as Elijah Muhammad's representative.

Act of 1964 but expressed concern over evidence of continuing racism in America. Although the resolution carried no authority, Malcolm proclaimed it a victory.

Malcolm had plans beyond the non-binding resolution of the OAU. He hoped to have the OAU bring the issue of the white man's treatment of American blacks to the attention of the world through the United Nations. He wanted to have the United States charged before the international body with violating the human rights of Afro-Americans. He argued that racism in South Africa was not considered just a domestic problem, but an international one. He argued that the world did not view the Soviet Union's treatment of its Jewish population as a domestic problem. Neither, he argued, should racism in America be considered a domestic problem.

The U.S. government did not appreciate Malcolm's activities at the OAU conference. Washington officials asked the Justice Department to consider prosecuting Malcolm for violation of the Logan Act, which forbids private citizens from communicating with foreign powers for the purpose of thwarting established policies of the federal government.

Exactly how great a threat Malcolm posed to American interests overseas is debated. Although Malcolm was investigated by the U.S. Central Intelligence Agency (CIA), there is no record of any charges filed against him in connection with his OAU activities. Some scholars believe that federal officials viewed his plan to bring America's racial issue before the United Nations as a serious threat to the country's interests overseas. Other scholars contend that the African nations Malcolm contacted would never have risked losing American financial aid by voting against the United States in the United Nations. They acknowledge that the U.S. government may have considered Malcolm X to be an irritant and an embarrassment, but they dismiss the idea that Malcolm was viewed as a serious threat.

An Important Step

Along with his OAU activities, Malcolm continued his efforts to reinvent himself and define a philosophy that stood apart from the Nation of Islam. On October 4, 1964, the *New York Times* published excerpts of a letter Malcolm had written from Mecca to a friend. In the letter, dated September 22, Malcolm renounced his old position of black racism and declared himself "a Muslim in the most orthodox sense."

> This religion recognizes all men as brothers. It accepts all human beings as equals before God, and as equal members in the Human Family of Mankind. I totally reject Elijah Muhammad's racist philosophy, which he has labeled "Islam" only to fool and misuse gullible people, as he fooled and misused me. But I blame only myself, and no one else for the fool that I was, and the harm that my evangelic foolishness in his behalf has done to others. . . .
>
> I respect every man's right to believe whatever his intelligence leads him to believe is intellectually sound . . . and I respect my right to believe likewise.[39]

Although in part politically motivated, Malcolm's letter was an important step in his evolution as a black leader. In plain language, he replaced racism with respect for all of humanity. Without committing himself to any specific strategy, his words hinted at a new, positive direction that would benefit people of all races.

But Malcolm could not extend his newfound respect to his old mentor. In the same letter, he denounced Elijah Muhammad as a "religious faker" and declared "I shall never rest until I have undone the harm I did to so many well-meaning, innocent Negroes who through my own evangelistic zeal now believe in him even more fanatically and more blindly than I did."[40] The statement only deepened the acrimony between Malcolm and the Nation.

Looking Back

As 1964 drew to a close, Malcolm must have reviewed the year with mixed feelings. He had broken with Elijah Muhammad in March and formed the Muslim Mosque, Inc. To disassociate himself from his old image, he had undertaken a hajj to Mecca. He had taken steps to develop ties between blacks in America and Africa. He had conceived a bold plan to bring the plight of American blacks before the United Nations.

But at the same time, he had struggled with little success to define a new political position that appealed both to his old supporters and to more moderate American blacks. His Muslim Mosque, Inc. had grown little during the year. He was forced to recognize that his plan to bring the United States before the United Nations had little support among Ameri-

Author Alex Haley holds a copy of his best-selling book Roots. *Before he became widely known for* Roots, *he helped Malcolm X write his autobiography.*

can blacks. In addition, throughout the year he had been engaged in an increasingly bitter feud with Elijah Muhammad and his followers.

Malcolm had made many enemies, and as the year closed, he sensed that he was in danger. Throughout the past two years, Malcolm had been meeting periodically with writer Alex Haley to dictate his autobiography. Now, as the book neared completion, Malcolm asked Haley to give him a copy of the manuscript to read. He was convinced that he would not live to see the story of his life in print.

Chapter

7 The Assassination

As the year 1965 began, Malcolm attempted to push ahead with his efforts to build support at home and abroad. He continued his feud with the Nation of Islam, seemingly determined to expose Elijah Muhammad to the world. But the strain of the past year had taken a toll. He felt the world closing in on him. Within sixty days, he was dead. Those who mourned and those who hated Malcolm X would study the final days of his life in search of clues to the mystery surrounding his death.

During a 1964 press conference, Malcolm X predicts racial violence. A year later, a more moderate Malcolm found the press couldn't shake their violent image of him.

Trapped

In the months since his split with the Nation of Islam, Malcolm had struggled to find support among the black people of the United States. His speeches throughout the year had included both militant and moderate statements, as he attempted to broaden his appeal. But Malcolm had encountered as much frustration as success in his efforts to reinvent himself. In early January, he expressed his frustrations to Alex Haley, who recalled their conversation in the Epilogue of *The Autobiography of Malcolm X:*

> He talked about the pressures on him everywhere he turned, and about the frustrations, among them that no one wanted to accept anything relating to him "except my old 'hate' and 'violence' image." He said "the so-called moderate" civil rights organizations avoided him as "too militant" and the "so-called militants" avoided him as "too moderate." "They won't let me turn the corner!" he once exclaimed. "I'm caught in a trap."[41]

An undefined image was not the only trap Malcolm seemed to be caught in. His feud with the Nation of Islam had turned

Malcolm encourages a group of black Alabama youth to fight for their civil rights and not to settle for second-class citizenship.

into a war. Although both Malcolm and Elijah Muhammad seemed to be upset by the split, neither could or would stop it. Malcolm was intent on exposing the immorality of Elijah Muhammad and discrediting the Nation of Islam. The Nation seemed to be intent on stopping him. On January 28, Malcolm flew to Los Angeles to meet with the lawyer representing two secretaries who were filing lawsuits claiming that Elijah Muhammad had fathered their children. Malcolm was shadowed by Nation members throughout his stay. On the way to the airport, a speeding car pulled even with Malcolm's taxi. Malcolm stuck a cane out the window, as though it were a rifle, and the car veered away.

Malcolm flew to Chicago, where he met with members of the Illinois Attorney General's office, which was investigating alleged improprieties in the complex finances of the Nation of Islam. Throughout

his stay, Malcolm remained under police guard. Everywhere he went, he saw members of the Nation lurking nearby. Malcolm remarked to an associate that the Nation seemed to know every move he made.

On February 4, Malcolm traveled to Selma, Alabama, the site of a voting rights drive organized by the Southern Christian Leadership Conference. The SCLC leader, Dr. Martin Luther King Jr., had been jailed before Malcolm's arrival. Malcolm spoke only briefly, saying that he did not advocate violence, but neither did he advocate nonviolence. He told a reporter that he was for freedom, "by whatever means necessary." Although Malcolm did not meet Dr. King, he spoke briefly with Martin's wife. He told Coretta Scott King that he was not there to make trouble but to offer whites a glimpse of the alternative they might have to deal with if they did not accept Dr. King's program. His comments to Mrs. King seemed to indicate that Malcolm had come close to carving out a role for himself in the civil rights movement. He believed that he could use the image of violence that persistently accompanied him to force the white establishment to be more receptive to Dr. King's more moderate civil rights program.

Trouble Abroad

From Selma, Malcolm shifted his attention to increasing his support abroad. On February 5, he left for speaking engagements in London and Paris to promote his agenda for internationalizing the struggle of black people. He spoke at the First Congress of the Council of African Organizations in London on February 8. The next day, he flew to Paris, where he

A tense, wary Malcolm X in front of his house after it had been firebombed.

planned to speak at the Federation of African Students. But Malcolm was turned away at the airport and forced to return to London. In London, he talked via telephone with Afro-Cuban nationalist Carlos Moore, who had been waiting for him in Paris. Malcolm sensed a conspiracy behind the French government's refusal to let him enter the country:

> I was surprised when I turned up at Paris and got off the plane and was arrested, since I thought if there was any country in Europe that was liberal in its approach to things, France was it, so I was shocked when I got there and couldn't land. They wouldn't even give me any excuse or explanation. At first I thought it was the American State Department. The only other answer is that France has become a satellite of Washington, D.C.[42]

Malcolm returned to America. The French government later stated that Mal-

colm had been refused entry because his safety could not be guaranteed. Whether the French had acted independently or under covert pressure from the United States remains undetermined.

Fire in the Night

Malcolm's troubles continued upon his return to New York. In the early morning hours of February 14, as Malcolm and his family slept in their home in the East Elmhurst section of Queens, a blast shattered the dark. The family's house had been firebombed. Malcolm and his wife Betty, who was pregnant, snatched up the children and marshalled them outside the burning house. The fire department battled the flames for an hour, but the house was destroyed. Malcolm had no fire insurance. The fire left the family with few possessions and no money.

The fire was an eerie parallel to the fire that had ravaged Malcolm's childhood home in Lansing, Michigan. The parallel became all the more bizarre when speculation arose that Malcolm had set the fire himself as a "publicity stunt," or to destroy the house before the court evicted him at the Nation's request. A tin of gasoline on the dresser in the bedroom of one of Malcolm's children was cited as evidence that Malcolm had set the fire.

An incensed Malcolm denied the charge that he would endanger his own family by setting fire to their house. He charged that the gasoline tin had been planted by the police or fire department. The day after the fire, he spoke at the Audubon Ballroom, blaming the fire-bombing on the Black Muslims and Elijah Muhammad. He called the Messenger "insane."

In the days after the fire, Malcolm began to have second thoughts about his original charge that the Nation had bombed his house in an attempt on his life. He recalled a violent illness he had experienced the preceding August in Cairo and wondered whether he had been poisoned. He thought about the French government's refusal to admit him to that country and asked himself who might have been behind it. In a conversation with Alex Haley, he confessed his doubts:

> You know, I'm going to tell you something, brother—the more I keep thinking about this thing, the things that have been happening lately, I'm not all that sure it's the Muslims. I know what they can do, and what they can't, and they can't do some of the stuff recently going on. Now, I'm going to tell you, the more I keep thinking about what

happened to me in France, I think I'm going to quit saying it's the Muslims.[43]

Although it was obvious that someone had set the fire, the police made little effort to find out who was responsible. The identity of the arsonist remains a mystery.

Death in Harlem

Despite the fire, and despite his fears, Malcolm pressed on. A week after the fire, he had scheduled a rally of the OAAU at the Audubon Ballroom in Harlem. On February 21, a Sunday, he arrived at the ballroom shortly before two o'clock in the afternoon. He told an associate that he was going to say he had been hasty in blaming the Black Muslims for fire-bombing his home. He seemed preoccupied and irritable. He became furious when he learned that the other speakers had canceled their appearances.

Scattered and overturned chairs in Harlem's Audubon Ballroom are the only evidence of the brief but deadly violence that ended the life of Malcolm X.

The 1965 national convention of the Nation of Islam listens to Elijah Muhammad's speech denying that the Nation had any part in the assassination of Malcolm X.

Benjamin X Goodman (who later took the Islamic name Benjamin Karim) had been Malcolm's assistant for eight years. In his own memoir, Brother Benjamin recalled that until that afternoon he had not "seen Malcolm more distraught than he had been upon learning of Mr. Muhammad's infidelities, when he had felt as if his brain cells were bleeding. . . . Malcolm's soul could not bear much more," Brother Benjamin thought, as Malcolm vented his fury.[44]

A few minutes later, Brother Benjamin preceded Malcolm to the stage to warm up the crowd. He spoke for a half-hour, then introduced Malcolm. Malcolm took his position behind the podium. His wife Betty and their children were in the audience. He gave his traditional greeting. "Asalaikum, brothers and sisters"—peace be unto you. In the audience, about 400 people shifted in their seats, ready to hear Malcolm's message.

Brother Benjamin, who had just gone backstage, recalled what happened next:

Just as he was about to begin his address, a man near the center of the audience started a commotion. Pushing back his chair, he leapt up and said loudly to the person next to him, "Nigger, get your hand out of my pocket!" On top of the accusation, from the same area, came a few rapid shots that sounded like firecrackers. "Hold it!" Malcolm shouted from the podium; you can hear it on the tape of the rally. "Hold it!" he shouted into the blasts of gunfire not fifteen feet away from him. A bullet cut through Malcolm's microphone. He reeled back, he fell. It had happened in a matter of seconds.[45]

Panic broke out. Men and women dropped to the floor. People rushed to the stage to attend Malcolm, but he seemed to be beyond help. An ambulance was summoned. He was taken to Vanderbilt Clinic of Columbia-Presbyterian Hospital. At 3:30 P.M., a hospital spokesperson made the terrible announcement that Malcolm X was dead.

The news stunned all of Harlem. Mourners gathered outside the Hotel Theresa, the headquarters of the OAAU. They were quietly dispersed late in the afternoon. Throughout Harlem, a sense of gloom hung in the February air.

The Monday papers carried the story on the front page. An editorial in the *New York Times* described Malcolm as "an extraordinary and twisted man, turning many true gifts to evil purpose." Elsewhere in the paper, the nation's black leaders reacted to Malcolm's death. Dr. Martin Luther King Jr. said:

> We must face the tragic fact that Malcolm X was murdered by a morally inclement climate. It revealed that our society is still sick enough to express dissent through murder. We have not learned to disagree without being violently disagreeable. This vicious assassination should cause our whole society to see that violence and hatred are evil forces that must be cast into unending limbo.[46]

Newsweek titled its coverage of the assassination "Death of a Desperado,"[47] a headline that inappropriately classified Malcolm as some kind of fleeing criminal. In Africa, the nations Malcolm had lobbied for support in his efforts to internationalize the struggle of black people paid tribute to him in newspaper articles and editorials.

Malcolm's death did not end the violence. Some of his associates pledged revenge. Late Monday night, a firebomb was thrown into the Nation of Islam's New York mosque. The next day, another fire was set in the Nation's San Francisco mosque.

On Tuesday evening, the Unity Funeral Home opened its doors to mourners. Over the next few days, amidst tight security marred by a bomb threat, more than 22,000 people filed by Malcolm's casket to pay their respects.

On Friday, Sheik Ahmed Hassoun, who had become Malcolm's spiritual adviser and was to teach at the Muslim Mosque, arrived at the funeral home. He removed Malcolm's western clothing and draped him in the traditional seven white linen burial shrouds known as the kafan.

That same day, halfway across the nation in Chicago, an emotional Elijah Muhammad spoke at the Savior's Day convention of the Nation of Islam. Frail and in poor health, he gasped for breath at the podium. His followers urged him to take his time. Elijah Muhammad denied any role in the assassination and said that Malcolm had gone astray. "We are innocent of Malcolm's death," he insisted. "Malcolm died of his own preaching. He preached violence, and violence took him away."[48] He told his followers that he would not let "crackpots" like Malcolm destroy what Allah had sent to the Nation.

Mourners, police, and the press gather at the entrance to Faith Temple in New York as Malcolm X's casket is carried to a waiting hearse.

At the cemetery, Malcolm's wife, accompanied by various civil rights leaders, bids her husband a final farewell.

On Saturday, the day of the funeral, mourners began to gather outside the Church of Faith Temple early in the morning. By nine o'clock an estimated 6,000 were standing behind barricades, peering from nearby windows, or shivering on fire escapes.

The service started with the reading of telegrams of condolence from civil rights leaders and from governments abroad. There were words of praise from Omar Osman, a representative of the Islam Center of Switzerland and the United States. Then actor and activist Ossie Davis stood and delivered a eulogy: "He was and is—a Prince—our own black shining Prince! . . . who didn't hesitate to die, because he

loved us so."[49] There were other brief speeches. The family filed by Malcolm's coffin for the final time.

The funeral cortege traveled eighteen miles to the Ferncliff Cemetery. There the man who had reinvented himself many times, the man known through the years as Malcolm Little, Homeboy, Detroit Red, Satan, Malcolm X, and El-Hajj Malik El-Shabazz, was laid to rest.

Who Killed Malcolm X?

Although a crowd of around 400 people witnessed the assassination, who killed Malcolm X and why has never been completely and satisfactorily explained. The killing is assumed to be the work of hired assassins, but who hired them and why remains the subject of controversy almost three decades after Malcolm's death.

Immediately after the shots were fired, audience members captured one black man. He was wounded in the leg by a bullet fired from the gun of one of Malcolm's security guards. The man was arrested by a police officer, hustled into a police car, and taken to police headquarters by two other policemen. The suspect was identified as Talmadge Hayer, also known by the name Thomas Hagen.

Several days after Malcolm's death, two Black Muslims, Thomas 15X Johnson (later known as Kahil Islam) and Norman 3X Butler (later Muhammad Abdul Aziz) were arrested and charged with Malcolm's assassination.

Despite grand jury testimony by Benjamin X Goodman and other evidence that Johnson and Butler were not even at the Audubon Ballroom the afternoon

Malcolm was killed, they along with Talmadge Hayer were indicted and brought to trial early in 1966.

During the trial, Hayer suddenly confessed his role in the assassination. He admitted shooting Malcolm. He denied that Thomas 15X Johnson and Norman 3X Butler were involved, but refused to name anyone else. The jury determined that Hayer was only covering for his codefendants. All three were convicted and sent to prison for life on March 12, 1966.

The case was officially closed, but important questions remained unanswered. If Hayer's claim that Johnson and Butler were not involved was true, then who were the other shooters? Who had hired them?

Eleven years after Johnson, Butler, and Hayer went to prison, new information surfaced. In affidavits filed in November

Norman Butler was one of three men arrested for allegedly taking part in the murder of Malcolm X. The three were later convicted.

1977 and February 1978, Talmadge Hayer cleared Butler and Johnson of any involvement in Malcolm's murder. He gave the first names of four members of the Newark, New Jersey, mosque as the other hired assassins. They were "Leon X," "William X," "Wilbur," and "Ben." Neither the accused nor anyone else has come forward with evidence to corroborate Hayer's new account of the assassination.

Hayer, Butler, and Johnson were paroled from prison in the mid-1980s. Although most people now believe that Butler and Johnson are innocent, officially they have never been cleared of the murder conviction.

Conspiracy Theories

Although Hayer's affidavits named four other assassins, thus indirectly linking the Nation of Islam to Malcolm's death, Hayer did not satisfactorily explain who had instructed the five men to kill Malcolm. Exactly who ordered Malcolm to be killed and why remains a mystery. Those who have studied Malcolm's life and the assassination have formed several conspiracy theories.

The most commonly accepted theory is that Malcolm X fell victim to his rivalry with the Nation of Islam. Those who support this theory believe that members of the Nation of Islam killed Malcolm because he was trying to discredit Elijah Muhammad and the movement. As evidence, they document other cases in which the Nation dealt with its rivals through violence. Hayer and the other assassins he named all had ties to the Nation of Islam. Whether they were acting independently, were hired by higher Muslim officials, or were hired directly or indirectly by the Messenger himself, remains unanswered.

Others argue that those who hired Hayer and the others were only exploiting the feud between Malcolm and the Nation of Islam as a cover. They argue that instead of being killed in a power struggle between two black organizations, Malcolm X was murdered because he challenged and threatened white society. The assassination was made to look like the work of the Nation of Islam. Malcolm himself had fueled this theory before his death by saying he believed he was being pursued by forces greater than the Nation of Islam.

Alternately, those who believe that Malcolm was killed by forces greater than the Nation of Islam have linked the New York City Police Department, the Federal Bureau of Investigation (FBI), and the Central Intelligence Agency to Malcolm's death. All these agencies had investigated

Malcolm X and his activities, in some cases infiltrating his organizations. From these investigations, people have derived various motives that might have resulted in Malcolm's death.

One theory charges that the New York City police were involved in Malcolm's death. According to this theory, the police feared that Malcolm was becoming too influential and threatened the peace of New York City. Although it was well known that Malcolm's life had been threatened by the Nation of Islam, there were only two policemen on duty in the Audubon Ballroom when Malcolm was killed. Police maintained that Malcolm had declined additional security, a statement that conflicts with claims by Malcolm's associates that he had complained about the lack of police protection. The police, some maintain, deliberately stayed away from the Audubon Ballroom the day Malcolm was killed.

Controversy surrounds the events immediately after the shots were fired. Early

Reporters and photographers crowd around Elijah Muhammad at a press conference given by the Muslim leader after Malcolm's death.

No Government Conspiracy

Michael Friedly, in Malcolm X: The Assassination, *concludes that while various government agencies were guilty of misdeeds, none was directly responsible for assassinating Malcolm X.*

"But the argument of conspiracy theorists that the [New York Police Department], as well as the FBI and the CIA, were directly involved in the murder of Malcolm X is misdirected. All three government agencies have a number of questions to answer in terms of their relationships to Malcolm X, but they are of a far less serious nature than whether or not they murdered a major figure in the African-American struggle for equality. The CIA must answer to charges that it spied on him overseas. The FBI must explain its surveillance of the Muslim leader and whether it played a role in exacerbating the split between him and Elijah Muhammad. And the New York Police Department must open its files and provide more information on why it was unable to protect Malcolm X despite the obvious threats to his life.

Perhaps one explanation of this treatment of government agencies toward a major African-American figure of his time is that, as Malcolm X said repeatedly, blacks were only second-class citizens, if they were actually citizens at all. 'The founding fathers—the ones who said "liberty or death" and all those pretty-sounding speeches—were slave owners themselves,' Malcolm X often shouted as he tried to incite his audiences to support his calls for a separate nation within the United States. 'When they said "liberty," they didn't mean the black man. They meant the white people.'"

newspaper accounts state that two suspects were apprehended near the scene of the shooting, but later editions report that only one suspect was taken into police custody. Some people claim the New York City police rescued an undercover agent immediately after the shooting, which would explain the sudden "disappearance" of the second suspect. Most critics discount this claim, saying that the newspapers mistakenly interpreted accounts of Hayer's arrest from two police officers as relating to two separate suspects, an error corrected in later editions.

Another theory implicates the FBI in Malcolm's death. The FBI had monitored the Nation of Islam and Malcolm since the early 1950s. After his split with the Nation

An Assassin's Motive

In an affidavit filed in November 1977, convicted assassin Talmadge Hayer described the motive that he says led him and four other members of the Newark mosque to kill Malcolm X. In this selection from Michael Friedly's Malcolm X: The Assassination, *the spelling and punctuation are Hayer's.*

"These brothers asked me what I thought about the situation with Mal. X? I said I thought it was very bad for anyone to go against the teachings of the Hon. Elijah, then known as the Last Messenger of God. I was told that Muslims should more or less be willing to fight against hypocrites and I agreed [with] that. There was no money payed to me for my part in this. I thought I was fighting for truth & right. There was a few meetings held concerning this. Sometimes these were held in a car driving around. Bro. Lee, Bro. Ben, a Brother named Willie X, the other Brother's name was Willbour or a name like it. From these meetings it was decided that the only place that Mal. X. was sure to be was the Audubon Ballroom on Feb. 21, 1965. Therefore the plan was to kill this person there. On Feb. 21st 1965 we met at Bens house Sunday morning. On Feb 20th 1965 we had gone to the Ballroom to check it out."

of Islam, Malcolm was kept under increasing surveillance. The FBI, this theory says, feared that the charismatic Malcolm might become a "black messiah" who would rise up from the ghetto and lead a black revolution in America. According to this theory, Malcolm was killed because he was a potential threat to the nation's peace. Most people discount this interpretation of the assassination.

Others believe that Malcolm's growing international status was a factor in his death. Malcolm's efforts to have the race issue in America taken up by the United Nations were viewed by some U.S. government officials as a threat to the nation's interests overseas. In this theory, Malcolm was killed to prevent him from continuing to work toward a UN vote. Supporters of this theory point to Malcolm's illness in Cairo in 1964 as further evidence of a government plot, noting that Malcolm himself had raised the possibility of poisoning.

As with the assassinations of Abraham Lincoln, John F. Kennedy, Robert F. Kennedy, Martin Luther King Jr., and many others, no single theory answers every question or accounts for every shred of evidence unearthed over the years. Even if an explanation could be found that satisfied everyone, it would not bring Malcolm X back. Both a product and a victim of the society in which he was born, Malcolm X died before he could use his remarkable talents to help find a solution to America's racial problems.

8 A Complex Legacy

Nearly three decades after his death, Malcolm X is more popular than he ever was during his lifetime. His strong, defiant face stares out at America from T-shirts, sweatshirts, jackets, and posters. Baseball caps bearing the unmistakable "X" are worn proudly by America's black youth. Malcolm's speeches are sampled in music by leading rap artists of today. In the fall of 1992, a movie about his life broke the opening-day box office record in America's theaters.

In marketing terms, Malcolm X is hot. But the products are only the most visible part of a complex legacy left behind by a very complicated man. Although the Muslim Mosque, Inc., and the Organization of Afro-American Unity, the two organizations he founded in the year before his death quickly withered, Malcolm X remains as important today as he was a generation ago. Long after Malcolm's image and "X" cease to be fashion statements, scholars and admirers

Young blacks wearing Malcolm X and Spike Lee T-shirts walk in a funeral procession on a New York street.

A man invokes the legacy of Malcolm X as he pickets outside a Chicago business.

will continue to discuss the man's legacy and its relevance to the changing times.

A Voice of Anger and Pride

Although Malcolm X represents many things to different people, the most significant and enduring part of his legacy is the unique voice he gave to black America. Throughout America's history there have been black leaders who have fought racism, but none like Malcolm X. His extremist message stood apart from the voices of other black leaders of his time. Rather than trying to "make friends" with white people, Malcolm "told off" white people to their faces. Casting off the cloak of subservience his race had worn for three centuries, Malcolm fearlessly spoke out loud the frustrations and anger that black people throughout America were afraid to express about their experiences in a white-dominated society.

But beyond merely articulating the anger and frustration of the times, Malcolm voiced some sharp observations about American society. He said that whites would never consider black people to be their equal. He also pointed out that the promise that blacks could advance by trying to be white was an illusion. Knowing this, he told black people that they had to help themselves, "by any means necessary," rather than wait for whites to change.

In place of subservience, Malcolm offered black Americans a sense of pride. He helped redefine an entire race in terms of themselves, rather than with respect to white people. The slogans "black pride" and "black is beautiful," which became popular after Malcolm's death, nourished the feelings of pride he helped initiate. When Malcolm was growing up, people of color were called Negroes—or worse. Malcolm helped strip away these old labels and the subservient attitudes that accompanied them. As *Newsweek* reported in late 1992: "It was Malcolm who insisted that blacks start calling themselves 'Afro-Americans,' as a symbol of pride in their roots and a spur to learn more about their history."[50] In paying tribute to Malcolm's importance, *U.S. News & World Report* noted the belief of many scholars that Malcolm X's influence "turned 'Negroes' into 'black people.'"[51]

Ossie Davis was referring to Malcolm's willingness to "talk back" to white people and the pride in being black that he communicated when he said, "Malcolm was our manhood, our living black manhood."[52]

It is ironic that Malcolm is idealized today because of his rage. In his own lifetime, people feared Malcolm's rage and the violence they associated with it. Although he was admired by many black people, many more felt he was too extreme. Malcolm was frequently overshadowed by other black leaders who preached nonviolence, in particular Dr. King. In a survey taken shortly before Malcolm died, only 6 percent of New York City's blacks

A black student responds with pride to a board on his school wall reminding blacks of their value as a people.

A black man in south central Los Angeles sports a Malcolm X T-shirt as he takes part in the 1992 riots.

considered Malcolm X their most effective leader. Seventy-five percent bestowed that honor on Martin Luther King Jr.

A survey conducted in November 1992 for *Newsweek* magazine, however, found that 57 percent of all blacks consider Malcolm a hero. Among black people ages fifteen through twenty-four, 84 percent regard him as a hero. Nearly thirty years after his death, Malcolm has equaled and perhaps surpassed Martin Luther King in popularity, particularly among young people. It is the words of Malcolm X, rather than Dr. King, that appear in songs of the leading rap artists of the nineties. Whereas Martin preached nonviolence, Malcolm told blacks to use any means necessary to achieve equality. Today many young, inner city blacks find Malcolm's message more relevant to their lives. To many, Martin's nonviolent approach has already failed.

Many scholars attribute Malcolm's rising popularity as a symbol of black anger to the continued existence of the racism he decried. Although many black people have made great progress in the decades since his death, throughout America, especially in the inner cities, many black people still suffer from discrimination. On the nation's streets, for example, young blacks are more likely to be stopped by police than young whites.

In addition, "complaints are mounting that a black person still can't eat in the same setting as a white,"[53] according to a recent newspaper article. In lawsuits filed against some of the nation's leading restaurant chains, black patrons "talk of special cover charges, of being forced to pre-pay for food, of waiting in line while whites are ushered ahead, of being refused advertised specials."[54] Black residents of the inner cities also complain that they remain shut out of better job opportunities, higher education, and decent housing.

Many scholars note that such discrimination remains one of America's most pressing problems. They point to the 1992 Los Angeles riots in the wake of the Rodney King verdict as dramatic evidence that black rage remains bottled up in the nation's inner cities.

Malcolmania

The relevance of Malcolm's message in the early 1990s planted the seeds for the rapid growth of a phenomenon one scholar calls "Malcolmania." Malcolmania is the fusion of a continuing tradition of honoring Malcolm X and a recent effort to use Malcolm's popularity to sell all kinds of merchandise.

Although Malcolm's name all but disappeared from the popular media after his death, among scholars and admirers his influence never really faded. Malcolm's name became familiar to a new generation of students who studied black history and culture in college. In the late 1980s, Malcolm's image began popping up on T-shirts, and before long, a new market was born. *Forbes,* a national business magazine, recorded the irony of the marketability of Malcolm's militant message.

A poster of Malcolm X with the word "freedom" scrawled across the bottom is propped in front of a vehicle burned during the 1992 Los Angeles riots.

Malcolm X, the fiery black activist, said he'd achieve his goals "by any means necessary." He probably never expected those means would include licensed T-shirts, jewelry, baseball caps, mugs, posters, sunglasses, board games, and potato chips.

Today Malcolm X's image has become as hot as his rhetoric was. Retail sales of licensed Malcolm X products, all emblazoned with a large "X," could reach $100 million this year, according to Curtis Management Group, which manages licensing for Malcolm's estate.[55]

Ironically, while this marketing blitz increased Malcolm's popularity, some black leaders fear it has oversimplified the importance of a complex leader. A T-shirt image or "X" baseball cap, black leaders worry, reduces Malcolm X to a single symbol.

As a commodity, the complexity of Malcolm has simply been flattened. He's like a statue in a museum, which if you turn this way you see one side of him, and if you turn that way you see another side; and each side that you see reflects something that you want to have affirmed in yourself. That which does not please you, or provokes anxiety or discomfort in you, you turn away from, you ignore. I think that what we are seeing in the flattened images of Malcolm on T-shirts or even reduced more to simply the X, is the ridding of Malcolm's complexity, of his humanity, so that we can make use of him to affirm what we need in ourselves. But the danger—the great danger—in that is that what we see over and over again is Malcolm as the quintessential icon of Black rage.[56]

Scholars and educators fear that this single impression of Malcolm X is the extent of what far too many young people will learn about him. In some schools today studying hard to get good grades and advance is "out" among black students, replaced by a fatalistic sense of black identity. Peer pressure is so strong that some black students deliberately fail to study because they fear their friends will accuse them of trying to "act white." For this as well as other reasons, scholars fear young people will not take the time to read Malcolm's *Autobiography* or other books and articles about him. Thus, they will miss one of Malcolm's most important messages, namely the importance of getting an education.

Film director Spike Lee's movie biography of Malcolm X was a driving force in the resurgence of the late black leader's popularity.

A Message for Everyone

In an interview appearing in the November 23, 1992, issue of Time *magazine, film director Spike Lee addressed Malcolm's legacy.*

"Q. Why was making this movie so important to you?

A. Well, Malcolm is very important to me, and the reality is that young people—not just black but white kids also—don't read anymore. They get their information from movies, television, radio. So this is going to be a history lesson. This is going to open up the history book.

Q. Malcolm is revered by many young African Americans. Why is that?

A. I think that Ossie Davis put it best when he said, 'Malcolm is our shining black prince, our black manhood.' There's a void in that right now among young black males. And, you know, Malcolm's a great model. Public Enemy and KRS-One and Boogie Down Productions were not sampling 'I have a dream' in their songs, you know. It was Malcolm X.

Q. What do you think is Malcolm's primary legacy?

A. The main reason Malcolm X told his story to Alex Haley was to put his life up there as an example for African Americans—or anybody, really—that you could change your life around if you really apply yourself. He says, 'Look, people, I was a criminal. I peddled grass, I was a steerer, I was a criminal, I snorted cocaine. I got so depraved that even in prison, I was called Satan.' But he turned it around."

Malcolm X, the Movie

It was the need to bring the fuller range of Malcolm's legacy to a young population that spurred film director Spike Lee to turn *The Autobiography of Malcolm X* into a movie. A long-time admirer of Malcolm X, Lee felt he was "born" to make this movie. "I think that it really comes down to people having a very limited view of Malcolm, and not understanding that the man evolved, was constantly evolving, even at the time of the assassination,"[57] Lee told *Time* magazine in November 1992.

Others had attempted to make a movie about Malcolm X through the years and given up because of poor scripts, lack of financing, and fear that the public would not accept a drama about a militant black leader. Lee had established himself with several popular movies including *Do The Right Thing* and *Jungle Fever*. But he had to campaign hard to convince the movie industry and the black community that he could make the movie. Some members of the black community felt the young director was too self-indulgent to tell Malcolm's story "straight." Others thought that because of his success in Hollywood, Lee was becoming too far removed from the experience of inner city blacks to capture Malcolm's story on film.

But Lee prevailed and began his epic movie. If he had critics within the black community, he also had supporters. When the film went over budget and the studio refused to advance more money, black entertainers contributed money so that Lee could finish the movie.

Spike Lee's $33 million epic *Malcolm X* reached 1,124 of the nation's movie screens in November 1992. The movie set a box office record for opening day, taking in $2.4 million. As the nation flocked to movie theaters, the controversy continued. Director Lee was criticized for encouraging black students to skip school and attend the movie on opening day. He was also criticized for contributing to Malcolmania by merchandising thousands of "X" baseball caps.

The movie received mixed reviews. *U.S. News & World Report* noted "The movie is

---

Malcolm's Popularity Today

Newsweek *offered perspective on why Malcolm X is popular among today's black youth in the cover story of its November 16, 1992, issue.*

"If some young blacks now consider Malcolm X more of a hero than Martin Luther King, it's a testimony to both the success and the failure of King's dream. King's crusade for legal equality and greater opportunity has made life better for millions of blacks, allowing them to get better jobs, move to the suburbs and enjoy many of the same comforts that white Americans do. But that exodus has had the cruel effect of making those left behind—the kind of poor urban blacks who grew up like Malcolm— even worse off. One reason for Malcolm X's enduring appeal 'lies in the simple fact that we have not yet overcome,' says Duke University professor C. Eric Lincoln, who was a friend of Malcolm's. 'For many of the kids in the ghetto we are right back where we were. The few advances that have been made have not reached them. So if we didn't make it with King, what have we to lose? We might as well make it with Malcolm.'"

Nearly three decades after his death, Malcolm X has become a role model for young blacks. Some people, however, fear that too many youths will only model his early life of crime.

Malcolm X to a new generation and added to his legacy. The movie portrayed Malcolm as a role model for young people, continuing a tradition begun by the autobiography and by Malcolm's use of his own past in his speeches.

As a historical character, a character in a book, or a character in a movie, Malcolm X is a role model today for millions of black and white people. His life remains a remarkable, timeless story of triumph over adversity. He was born into poverty, grew up and slid into a street hustler's life, and went to prison. But with the right help at the right time, he channeled his rage and transformed himself from a convict into a moral, disciplined leader.

His story has the same ability to turn lives around as it did nearly thirty years ago. Reading *The Autobiography of Malcolm X,* according to *Newsweek,* helped to turn around the life of Los Angeles resident Ricky Troupe.

sure to shape and reshape the ways in which millions of people view a man who was one of his generation's plainest speaking, but most-misunderstood personalities."[58] But *Time* claimed that Lee had "elevated Malcolm's importance until the vital historical context is obscured."[59]

A Role Model

Despite the hype and criticism surrounding it, *Malcolm X* the movie introduced

At 15, [Ricky] Troupe came to L.A. as a ward of the court and all but dropped out of school and started to steal and deal drugs. One day he picked up *The Autobiography of Malcolm X.* "I was just going to read a little part of it," he says, "[but] I stayed up all night trying to finish that book." It gave Troupe hope that if Malcolm could emerge from the streets and turn his life around, so could he. He went back to school, and now, at 21, he's pulling A's in a paralegal program at a community college and hoping to get into a four-year program and eventually to law school. "I'm constantly setting high goals for myself," says Troupe. "That all ties into the effect Malcolm had on my life."[60]

By Any Means Necessary

Deidre Bailey expands the meaning of Malcolm's slogan "by any means necessary" in "The Autobiography of Deidre Bailey: Thoughts on Malcolm X and Black Youth," which appears in the anthology Malcolm X: In Our Own Image, *edited by Joe Wood.*

"I think we can find common ground. I know I say 'by any means necessary' all the time. But I don't use it to imply violence. I use it to imply that something has to be done and it's by any means necessary. The Rodney King verdict, for instance, made a lot of young people stop and think, 'Hey, this isn't about you and I beefing'—it's a racial issue. And that encompasses all black people and all minorities. Especially when you have blatant incidents like what happened to Rodney King. It wakes people up to what's really happening in our society. The best thing we can do is to try to work together, to try to come to some type of truce, because we have this big struggle ahead of us. 'By any means necessary' means I have to do whatever I can in my power to make sure this happens."

New Interpretations

Malcolm X was a complex man who stood for many things. Scholars and admirers who study his career, his speeches, and his autobiography continue to develop new insights about Malcolm and what he was trying to accomplish. Slowly, these insights are reaching the mainstream and broadening Malcolm's old image of militancy.

In his time, Malcolm's message was interpreted only as a call to violence. But unlike some militant black organizations that claimed to follow in his footsteps, Malcolm himself was not prone to violence. There are no known incidents of him actually committing violent acts to achieve his political goals. By recognizing the difference between his words and his deeds, scholars are beginning to interpret his message in broader terms. His famous call for advancement "by any means necessary," for example, has been expanded to mean obtaining an education, owning a business, or helping one another. Continued study of Malcolm's life will broaden the nation's understanding of a truly remarkable and gifted leader.

When Malcolm X was killed, he had not even reached the age of forty. He had been completely on his own for less than a year after breaking from the Nation of Islam. His tragic death deprived America of a remarkable mind that was still in a period of evolution and transition. Although his work had only begun, Malcolm's legacy will influence America for generations to come.

Notes

Introduction: "A Shining Black Prince"

1. Ossie Davis, "Our Shining Black Prince," in John Henrik Clarke, editor, *Malcolm X: The Man and His Times*. Trenton, NJ: African World Press, 1991, page xii.

2. Davis, "Eulogy," in John Henrik Clarke, editor, *Malcolm X: The Man and His Times*, page xii.

Chapter 1: Young Malcolm Little

3. Marcus Garvey, "The True Solution to the Negro Problem" (1922), in Francis L. Broderick and August Meier, editors, *Negro Protest Thought in the Twentieth Century*. New York: Bobbs-Merrill, 1965, page 85.

4. Garvey, "The True Solution to the Negro Problem" (1922), in Francis L. Broderick and August Meier, editors, *Negro Protest Thought in the Twentieth Century*, page 85.

5. Garvey, "The True Solution to the Negro Problem" (1922), in Francis L. Broderick and August Meier, editors, *Negro Protest Thought in the Twentieth Century*, page 83.

6. "Minister Malcolm: A Conversation with Kenneth B. Clark," in David Gallen, *Malcolm X: As They Knew Him*. New York: Carroll & Graf, 1992, page 132.

7. Bruce Perry, *Malcolm: The Life of a Man Who Changed Black America*. Barrytown, NY: Station Hill Press, 1991, page 9.

8. "Minister Malcolm: A Conversation with Kenneth B. Clark," in David Gallen, *Malcolm X: As They Knew Him*, page 133.

9. Malcolm X, *The Autobiography of Malcolm X*. New York: Grove, 1966, page 10.

10. "The Playboy Interview: Malcolm X Speaks with Alex Haley," in David Gallen, *Malcolm X: As They Knew Him*, page 122.

11. Perry, *Malcolm: The Life of a Man Who Changed Black America*, pages 39–40.

Chapter 2: Street Hustler

12. Perry, *Malcolm: The Life of a Man Who Changed Black America*, page 86.

13. Malcolm X, *The Autobiography of Malcolm X*, page 48.

14. Malcolm X, *The Autobiography of Malcolm X*, pages 54–55.

15. "The Playboy Interview: Malcolm X Speaks with Alex Haley," in David Gallen, *Malcolm X: As They Knew Him*, page 123.

16. Malcolm X, *The Autobiography of Malcolm X*, page 90.

17. Malcolm X, *The Autobiography of Malcolm X*, page 125.

Chapter 3: From Malcolm Little to Malcolm X

18. Malcolm X, *The Autobiography of Malcolm X*, page 156.

19. Malcolm X, *The Autobiography of Malcolm X*, page 164.

20. Malcolm X, *The Autobiography of Malcolm X*, pages 172–173.

21. "Malcolm X v. James Farmer: Separation v. Integration," in Francis L. Broderick and August Meier, editors, *Negro Protest Thought in the Twentieth Century*, page 358.

Chapter 4: Minister Malcolm X

22. Peter Goldman, *The Death and Life of Malcolm X.* Urbana: University of Illinois Press, 1979, pages 58–59.

23. Clayborne Carson, *Malcolm X: The FBI File.* New York: Carroll & Graf, 1991, page 170.

24. Perry, *Malcolm: The Life of a Man Who Changed Black America*, page 174.

25. "Minister Malcolm: A Conversation with Kenneth B. Clark," in David Gallen, *Malcolm X: As They Knew Him*, page 139.

26. "Martin Luther King Jr., 'I Have a Dream,'" in Francis L. Broderick and August Meier, editors, *Negro Protest Thought in the Twentieth Century*, page 403.

Chapter 5: A Split with Elijah Muhammad

27. Malcolm X, *The Autobiography of Malcolm X*, page 271.

28. Malcolm X, *The Autobiography of Malcolm X*, page 295.

29. Betty Shabazz, "Malcolm X as a Husband and Father," in John Henrik Clarke, editor, *Malcolm X: The Man and His Times*, page 140.

30. Malcolm X, *The Autobiography of Malcolm X*, page 309.

Chapter 6: His Own Man

31. "His Best Credentials: On the Air with Joe Rainey," in David Gallen, *Malcolm X: As They Knew Him*, page 156.

32. "His Best Credentials: On the Air with Joe Rainey," in David Gallen, *Malcolm X: As They Knew Him*, pages 156–157.

33. Perry, *Malcolm: The Life of a Man Who Changed Black America*, page 258.

34. "The Muslim Message: All White Men Devils, All Negroes Divine," *Newsweek*, August 27, 1962, page 27.

35. Malcolm X, *The Autobiography of Malcolm X*, pages 333–334.

36. Malcolm X, *The Autobiography of Malcolm X*, page 340.

37. *New York Times*, May 22, 1964, page 22.

38. "Organization of Afro-American Unity: A Statement of Basic Aims and Objectives" (New York, June 1964), in John Henrik Clarke, editor, *Malcolm X: The Man and His Times*, page 336.

39. *New York Times*, October 4, 1964, page 59.

40. *New York Times*, October 4, 1964, page 59.

Chapter 7: The Assassination

41. Alex Haley, "Epilogue," in Malcolm X, *The Autobiography of Malcolm X*, pages 423–424.

42. "Telephone Conversation," in John Henrik Clarke, editor, *Malcolm X: The Man and His Times*, page 205.

43. Haley, "Epilogue," in Malcolm X, *The Autobiography of Malcolm X*, pages 430–431.

44. Benjamin Karim, with Peter Skutches and David Gallen, *Remembering Malcolm.* New York: Carroll & Graf, 1992, pages 188–189.

45. Karim, with Peter Skutches and David Gallen, *Remembering Malcolm*, page 191.

46. *New York Times*, February 22, 1965, page 11.

47. *Newsweek*, March 8, 1965, page 24.

48. *Time*, March 5, 1965, page 25.

49. Davis, "Our Shining Black Prince," in John Henrik Clarke, editor, *Malcolm X: The Man and His Times*, 1991, page xii.

Chapter 8: A Complex Legacy

50. Mark Whitaker et al., "Malcolm X," *Newsweek*, November 16, 1992, page 70.

51. Lewis Lord and Jeannye Thornton, "The Legacy of Malcolm X," *U.S. News & World Report*, November 23, 1992, page 78.

52. Davis, "Our Shining Black Prince," in John Henrik Clarke, editor, *Malcolm X: The Man and His Times*, page xii.

53. Judy Pasternak, "Restaurant Sit-ins Long Past, but Blacks Still Await Service," *St. Paul Pioneer Press*, April 11, 1993, page 16A [reprinted from the *Los Angeles Times*].

54. Pasternak, "Restaurant Sit-ins Long Past, but Blacks Still Await Service," *St. Paul Pioneer Press*, April 11, 1993, page 16A.

55. R. Lee Sullivan, "Spike Lee versus Mrs. Malcolm X," in *Forbes*, October 12, 1992, page 136.

56. Ron Simmons and Marlon Riggs, "Sexuality, Television, and Death: A Black Gay Dialogue on Malcolm X," in Joe Wood, editor, *Malcolm X: In Our Own Image*. New York: St. Martin's Press, 1992, page 149.

57. Janice C. Simpson, "Words with Spike," *Time*, November 23, 1992, page 66.

58. Lord and Thornton, "The Legacy of Malcolm X," *U.S. News & World Report*, November 23, 1992, page 78.

59. Richard Corliss, "The Elevation of Malcolm X," *Time*, November 23, 1992, page 64.

60. Whitaker et al., "Malcolm X," *Newsweek*, November 16, 1992, page 70.

For Further Reading

Susan Altman, *Extraordinary Black Americans from Colonial to Contemporary Times.* Chicago: Childrens Press, 1989. This very readable book includes biographic essays on famous black Americans and essays on important themes in black history.

Nikki Grimes, *Malcolm X: A Force for Change.* New York: Fawcett Columbine, 1992. Targeted for middle-school readers, this volume covers Malcolm's entire life; the controversy surrounding his assassination is only briefly addressed, however.

Janet Harris, *The Long Freedom Road: The Civil Rights Story.* New York: McGraw-Hill, 1967. Concentrates on the events of the civil rights movement of the 1950s and 1960s more than on the dynamic personalities of the movement's leaders.

James Haskins, *The Life and Death of Martin Luther King Jr.* New York: Beech Tree Books, 1977. Part 1 covers King's life and career. Part 2 discusses his assassination and the controversy surrounding convicted assassin James Earl Ray.

Mary Lawler, *Marcus Garvey.* New York: Chelsea House, 1988. Malcolm's father Earl Little was a follower of Marcus Garvey. This volume covers Garvey's life and career. Introductory essay by Coretta Scott King.

Patricia and Frederick McKissack, *The Civil Rights Movement in America from 1865 to the Present.* Chicago: Childrens Press, 1987. This well-illustrated text covers black American history after the Civil War. Includes the contributions of whites as well as blacks to the civil rights movement.

Louise Meriwether, *Don't Ride the Bus on Monday: The Rosa Parks Story.* Englewood Cliffs, NJ: Prentice-Hall, 1973. For younger audiences, this slim volume covers the Montgomery bus boycott of 1955, which began when Parks refused to give up her seat to a white rider.

Walter Dean Myers, *Malcolm X: By Any Means Necessary.* New York: Scholastic, 1993. This reverent biography rightly emphasizes Malcolm's legacy as a role model. However, it tends to shy away from hard details on Malcolm's shortcomings, his bitter conflict with the Nation of Islam, and the controversy surrounding his murder.

Della Rowland, *Martin Luther King Jr: The Dream of Peaceful Revolution.* Englewood Cliffs, NJ: Silver Burdett, 1990. A biography that emphasizes King's life and career and does not address his assassination in detail. Introduction by former Atlanta mayor Andrew Young.

Howard Smead, *The Afro-Americans.* New York: Chelsea House, 1989. Part of the publisher's People of North America series, this volume begins in Africa and covers Afro-American history to the present. Introductory essay by Senator Daniel Patrick Moynihan (D, NY).

Works Consulted

Books

Francis L. Broderick and August Meier, editors, *Negro Protest Thought in the Twentieth Century.* New York: Bobbs-Merrill, 1965. This anthology of protest essays by Afro-Americans representing the period 1895–1965 helps to place Malcolm X's ideas in a historical context of black protest.

Clayborne Carson, *Malcolm X: The FBI File.* New York: Carroll & Graf, 1991. Contains memos, media clippings, and other information from the FBI's files on Malcolm X. An overview by the author describes the FBI's twenty-year surveillance of Malcolm X. Introduction by Spike Lee, director of the film *Malcolm X.*

John Henrik Clarke, editor, *Malcolm X: The Man and His Times.* Trenton, NJ: African World Press, 1991. A collection of essays, speeches, and other materials that interpret the career of Malcolm X. Also includes speeches and conversations with Malcolm himself. Of note: Ossie Davis's eulogy, the Charter for the Organization of Afro-American Unity, and Malcolm's "Outline for Petition to the United Nations Charging Genocide for 22 Million Black Americans."

James H. Cone, *Martin & Malcolm & America: A Dream or a Nightmare.* Maryknoll, NY: Orbis Books, 1991. A sometimes forced comparative evaluation of the careers of Malcolm X and Martin Luther King Jr., which concludes that each man was moving toward the other's political position at the time of his death.

Karl Evanzz, *The Judas Factor: The Plot to Kill Malcolm X.* New York: Thunder's Mouth Press, 1992. A detailed exploration of the theory that the U.S. intelligence community assassinated Malcolm X in its effort to destroy the civil rights movement.

Michael Friedly, *Malcolm X: The Assassination.* New York: Carroll & Graf/Richard Gallen, 1992. A study of the assassination that concentrates on the role of the Nation of Islam, and the wrongful convictions of Norman 3X Butler and Thomas 15X Johnson.

David Gallen, *Malcolm X: As They Knew Him.* New York: Carroll & Graf, 1992. An anthology of pieces about Malcolm X, including oral remembrances and the famous May 1963 *Playboy* interview conducted by Alex Haley.

Benjamin Karim, with Peter Skutches and David Gallen, *Remembering Malcolm.* New York: Carroll & Graf, 1992. A memoir about Malcolm X by the assistant who introduced him moments before the shooting.

Spike Lee, with Ralph Wiley, *By Any Means Necessary: The Trial and Tribulations of the Making of Malcolm X.* New York: Hyperion, 1992. Film director Lee describes the making of the movie. Includes the film's script.

Bruce Perry, *Malcolm: The Life of a Man Who Changed Black America.* Barrytown, NY: Station Hill Press, 1991. Often attacked by Afro-Americans, this critical biography of Malcolm X, in the words of one reviewer, makes its subject "smaller than life." Perry's psychoanalytic interpretation strips away Malcolm's "living black manhood." Carefully researched and extensively documented, this biography, when read in tandem with Malcolm's own *Autobiography,* is particularly helpful in seeing how and perhaps why

Malcolm X reinvented himself in his autobiography.

Bruce Perry, editor, *Malcolm X: The Last Speeches.* New York: Pathfinder, 1989. Published versions of two speeches from 1963, two interviews from December 1964, and two speeches from February 1965, given during the last week of Malcolm's life.

X, Malcolm, with the assistance of Alex Haley, *The Autobiography of Malcolm X.* New York: Grove, 1966. Malcolm X died before this book telling his own story was published. An excellent overview of Malcolm's life. When read in combination with a biography, its exaggerations and omissions reveal fascinating insight into Malcolm's personality and motives.

Joe Wood, editor, *Malcolm X: In Our Own Image.* New York: St. Martin's, 1992. Fifteen Afro-American writers address Malcolm's legacy and what it means to African Americans today. Short on pithy quotes, but long on deep reflection, these densely written essays shed considerable light on the complex legacy of Malcolm X.

Articles and Periodicals

"A Rage in Hollywood," World Press Review, October 1991, page 40. This article reprinted from *L'Expresso*, a liberal Italian magazine, offers an outside perspective on Hollywood's handling of America's racial tensions.

Richard Corliss, "The Elevation of Malcolm X", *Time*, November 23, 1992, pages 64–65. This critical review of the movie *Malcolm X* accuses director Spike Lee of elevating Malcolm's importance "until the vital historical context is obscured."

"Death and Transfiguration," *Time,* March 5, 1965, pages 23–35. A contemporary account of Malcolm's assassination and an overview of his life.

"Death of a Desperado," *Newsweek*, March 8, 1965. Despite its notoriously inappropriate title, this contemporary account succinctly covers Malcolm's assassination and its immediate aftermath.

"Denzel Washington Stars as 'Malcolm X' in Spike Lee Film," *Jet*, November 30, 1992. This short article previews Spike Lee's movie about Malcolm X, offering comments by its star, Denzel Washington.

Michael Eric Dyson, "Who Speaks for Malcolm? The Writings of Just About Everybody," *New York Times Book Review*, November 29, 1992. A review of several recent books about Malcolm X, built around the thesis that Malcolm's ideas are so diverse that almost anyone can find something to embrace.

M.S. Handler, "Malcolm Rejects Racist Doctrine," *New York Times*, October 4, 1964, page 59. This article includes excerpts from a letter Malcolm wrote from Mecca on September 22, 1964. In the excerpts quoted, Malcolm renounces racism and labels Elijah Muhammad a faker. The tone of the excerpts suggests that the letter was as much a public relations effort as an announcement of a new direction in a letter to a friend.

Lewis Lord and Jeannye Thornton, with Alejandro Bodipo-Memba, "The Legacy of Malcolm X," *U.S. News & World Report*, November 23, 1992. Malcolm's legacy is discussed in this article published just before the release of the movie *Malcolm X.*

Thomas Mikelson, "Martin and Malcolm," *Christian Century*, November 6, 1991. The similarities, differences, and contributions of Malcolm X and Dr. Martin Luther King Jr., are highlighted in this article constructed around a review of James H. Cone's *Martin & Malcolm & America: A Dream or a Nightmare.*

"Malcolm X," *New York Times,* February 22, 1965, page 20. In commenting on Malcolm's assassination, this editorial dramatically documents how misunderstood Malcolm was in his own time, describing its subject as a "twisted man, turning many true gifts to evil purpose."

"Premier of 'Malcolm X' Rakes in 2.4 Million; Sets Opening Day Record," *Jet,* December 7, 1992, page 55. A brief report addressing the record ticket sales generated by the movie *Malcolm X* on its opening day.

Janice C. Simpson, "Words with Spike Lee," *Time,* November 23, 1992, page 66. An interview with film director Lee focused around his movie *Malcolm X.*

R. Lee Sullivan, "Spike Lee versus Mrs. Malcolm X," *Forbes,* October 12, 1992, page 136. The merchandising blitz spawned by renewed interest in Malcolm X is documented in this article.

"The Muslim Message: All White Men Devils, All Negroes Divine," *Newsweek,* August 27, 1962, pages 26–28. Mainstream example of what biographer Bruce Perry called "withering" press coverage that critically examined the Nation of Islam in the wake of the television series "The Hate That Hate Produced."

Anne Thompson, "Malcolm, Let's Do Lunch," *Mother Jones,* July/August 1991, pages 26–29, 57. This article chronicles the twenty-five-year struggle to bring the story of Malcolm X to the nation's movie screens.

Mark Whitaker et al., "Malcolm X," *Newsweek,* November 16, 1992, pages 66–72. A detailed, succinct overview of Malcolm's legacy, including comments from scholars and contemporary black leaders about the relevance of Malcolm X in the 1990s.

Index

Africa, 10, 35, 36, 76, 79
   Malcolm X's tour of, 73–74
   return of black people to, 15
Afro-Americans, 9, 74, 93
   see also blacks
Allah, 34, 37, 73
Allah, Messenger of. *See* Muhammad, Elijah
Amsterdam News, 47
Archie, West Indian, 29, 31, 45
Audubon Ballroom, 83, 86, 88
Autobiography of Deidre Bailey: Thoughts on Malcolm X and Black Youth, 30, 100
Autobiography of Malcolm X, The 9, 21, 65, 68, 74, 79, 80, 96, 97, 99
   on a major turning point, 20
   on first meeting Elijah Muhammad, 41
   on the conk and self-degradation, 24
   on true knowledge of blacks, 36

Bimbi, as influence on Malcolm X, 33–34
blacks
   African names of, 8, 42
   in Boston, 22
   change in, 54
   color and, 14
   hair style and, 24
   in Harlem, 26
   internationalism and, 76
   legacy of Malcolm X for, 92–96
   Malcolm's call to, 8

   Marcus Garvey's call to, 13–14
   Martin Luther King and, 56–57
   position of, 69–70
   segregation of, 11–12
   "true knowledge" of, 8, 35–40
Butler, Norman 3X (Muhammad Abdul Aziz), 86–87

Charlestown State Prison, 32, 40, 42
CIA (Central Intelligence Agency), 78, 88
civil rights act
   of 1866, 11
   of 1964, 78
Civil Rights March of 1963, 57, 59
civil rights movement
   criticism of, 60
   Martin Luther King and, 8–9, 55–57
   Nation of Islam and, 9, 56–58, 64, 69
   resurgence of, 51–54
Civil War, 10–11, 76
Clark, Kenneth B., 15, 57
Concord Reformatory, 34
Confederacy, 11
conk, 24
Council of African Organizations, 81

Davis, Ossie, 9, 86, 93
discrimination, 12, 15–16, 51, 94–95
Do the Right Thing, 98

Faisal, Prince, 73
Fard, Wallace D., 37
Farmer, James, 53
FBI (Federal Bureau of Investigation), 88–90
Forbes, 95
Foxx, Red, 27
France, 82
Fruit of Islam, 41, 47

Galamison, Milton, 71
Garvey, Marcus, 18
   founding of UNIA by, 13
   message to blacks, 13–14
Gohanna family, 18–19
Goldwater, Barry, 60
Goodman, Benjamin X, 84, 86
Great Depression, 17, 51
Great Mosque, 73

hajj. *See* Mecca, pilgrimage to
Hajj Committee Court, 72
Haley, Alex, 18, 46, 79, 80, 83
Harlem, 26–29, 31, 45, 47
   significance of, 26, 45
Harvard Law School Forum, 46
Hassoun, Sheik Ahmed, 85
Hate That Hate Produced, The (Mike Wallace television series), 49–50
Hayer, Talmadge (Thomas Hagen), 86–87
Hicks, James, 47
Hinton, Johnson, 47
hustlers, 27

integration, 8, 13, 52–54, 56, 71
   token, 60

Islam, Nation of, 71, 85, 89, 100
    assassination of Malcolm X and, 87–88
    effect on members of, 51
    fishing for recruits to, 43–44, 50–51
    founding of, 37
    jealousy of Malcolm in, 58, 61–63
    as known to whites, 49–50
    Malcolm's break with, 67–69
    Malcolm's first contact with, 34
    Malcolm's struggle with, 61–69, 78–81
    orthodox Muslims and, 71
    position on integration and separation, 53–54
    position on nonviolence of, 54–55
    size of, 51
    "true knowledge" as taught by, 8, 35–40, 44
Islam, teachings of, 34, 44, 45, 62–63
    orthodox, 71

Jarvis, Malcolm, 23, 31
Jet, 65
Jim Crow laws, 11
Johnson, Thomas 15X (Kahil Islam), 86–87
Jungle Fever, 98

Ka'aba, 73
Kennedy, John F., 65, 66, 90
Kennedy, Robert F., 90
King, Coretta Scott, 81
King, Dr. Martin Luther, 90, 93–94, 98
    1963 Civil Rights March and, 57

comparing and contrasting Malcolm X and, 55–57
criticism of, 57, 61
integration of races and, 8
Montgomery bus boycott and, 53–54, 55–56
on assassination of Malcolm X, 85
Selma voter registration drive and, 81
King, Rodney, 95, 100
Koran, 45
Ku Klux Klan, 11, 18, 54

Lee, Spike
    movies of, 97–99
Lincoln, Abraham, 11, 90
Little, Earl (father of Malcolm X), 19, 22, 33
    burning of Lansing house of, 16
    color and, 14
    death of, 16–17
    early life of, 13
    as follower of Marcus Garvey, 15–16, 18
Little, Ella (half-sister of Malcolm X), 19–20, 22, 29, 31, 34, 39
Little, Hilda (sister of Malcolm X), 16, 38
Little, Louise (mother of Malcolm X), 13, 16, 18
    color and, 14
    mental breakdown of, 19
Little, Malcolm. *See* X, Malcolm
Little, Philbert (brother of Malcolm X), 16, 34
Little, Reginald (brother of Malcolm X), 16, 34–35, 39, 63
Little, Wesley (brother of Malcolm X), 16
Little, Wilfred (brother of Malcolm X), 16, 40, 48

Little, Yvonne (sister of Malcolm X), 16
Logan Act, 78

Malcolmania, 95–96
Malcolm: The Life of a Man Who Changed Black America (Perry)
    on color and family, 14
    on conversion to Islam, 38
    on crime and rebellion, 22
    on gaining international support, 75
    on leaving the Nation of Islam, 67
    on prison life, 33
Malcolm X (movie), 97–99
Malcolm X: In Our Own Image (Wood)
    on "by any means necessary," 100
    on Malcolm X as role model, 30
Malcolm X: The Assassination (Friedly)
    on conspiracy theories, 89
    on Talmadge Hayer's motive, 90
Malcolm X: The Man and His Times (Clarke), 65
Mecca, 9, 74, 78, 79
    pilgrimage to, 71–73
Meredith, James, 60
Mississippi, University of, 60
Montgomery bus boycott, 52–54, 55–56
Moore, Carlos, 82
Muhammad, Elijah, 8–9, 34, 35, 37–42, 85, 87
    avoidance of political action by, 58
    financial status of, 62
    first sighting of, 40–41
    rejection of philosophy of, 78–80

relationship between Malcolm and, 43, 45, 61–68, 70
rumors about immorality of, 62–65
Muhammad, Herbert, 62
Muhammad Speaks, 62, 70
Muslim Mosque, Incorporated, 71, 73, 79, 85, 91
establishment of, 70
Muslims, Black. *See* Islam, Nation of

National Association for the Advancement of Colored People (NAACP), 12, 52, 75
Newsweek, 71, 85, 93, 94, 99
on the current popularity of Malcolm X, 98
New York City Police Department, 88–89
New York Times, 68, 75, 78, 85
nonviolence, 8, 52–54, 94, 100
Nation of Islam position on, 54–55
Norfolk Prison Colony, 34, 40
numbers, lottery, 29

Organization of African Unity (OAU), 76, 78
Organization of Afro-American Unity (OAAU), 78, 83
charter of, 76
Osman, Omar, 86

Parks, Rosa, 53
Perry, Bruce (biographer of Malcolm X), 14, 19, 21, 33, 50, 67, 75
Playboy interview (Haley), 46

Quran, 45

racism
in America, 10, 20
black, 50, 78–79
effect on Malcolm X of, 10
internationalism and, 78
struggle against, 9
railroads, 26–28
Rainey, Joe, 70
religion
attitude toward, 33
conversion to Islamic, 34–40
first exposure to "natural," 34
Roseland Ballroom, 19, 23, 25, 35

segregation
goal of ending, 13
southern states and legal, 11–12, 51
"Separation v. Integration" (Cornell University debate), 53
Shabazz, Betty (wife of Malcolm X), 48, 61, 65, 68, 83, 84
Shabazz, El-Hajj Malik El-. *See* X, Malcolm
Shorty, 23, 24
slavery
in America, 10–11, 36, 39, 76 .
names of blacks and, 8, 42
Small's Paradise, 26–28
Sophia, 25, 31
Southern Christian Leadership Conference (SCLC), 52, 75, 81
Student Nonviolent Coordinating Committee (SNCC), 52
Swerlein, Mrs., 19

Time, 97, 99
Troupe, Ricky, 99

United Nations, 75–77, 79
United Negro Improvement Association (UNIA)
Earl Little and, 15–16
message of, 13–14
U.S. government, 78, 82, 90
U.S. News & World Report, 93, 98–99
Urban League, 75

Wallace, Mike, 49
"Where Is the American Negro Headed?" (television program), 56
white people, 57
African names stolen by, 8, 42
brotherliness of Islamic, 72
Martin Luther King and, 56–57
racist attitudes of, 10, 20
viewed as devils, 8, 34–35, 37, 44, 50, 74
World War II, 25, 51

X, Malcolm
ambition of, 45
assassination of, 9, 84–85
arrests and trial in, 86–87
conspiracy theories in, 87–90
birth of, 10
break with Nation of Islam of, 67–69
childhood of, 13–19
civil rights movement and, 55–57, 60–61, 64, 69, 81
color attitudes in family of, 14, 18

comparing and contrasting
Martin Luther King
and, 55–57
death threats against, 68
discovery of "true Islam"
by, 71–74
drugs and, 23, 28
education of, 18–19, 34–35,
37–40
as El-Hajj Malik El-Shabazz,
73
Elijah Muhammad and,
40–41, 43, 45, 58,
61–68, 70, 78–80, 85,
87
firebombing of New York
house of, 82–83
as founder of OAAU, 76
goal of, 42
in Harlem, 25–29, 31

Hinton incident and, 47
ideas of, 27, 44, 56, 69–70,
78
image as moderate and
militant of, 70–71, 76,
80, 81
influence of, 9
international work of,
73–76, 78, 81–82
legacy of, 91–100
marriage and family of,
48–49
Mecca pilgrimage of, 71–73
as member of Nation of
Islam, 40–68
in disagreement, 58–68
as minister, 44–45
as organizer, 45
as second-in-command,
59, 61

as spokesperson, 50,
59–60
name changed to, 42
in prison, 29, 31–35,
37–40
rejection of black racism
by, 78–79
religious conversion of, 21,
34–40
as role model, 30, 99
separation of races and, 8,
53–54
as street hustler, 21–31
summary of life of, 8–9
women and, 47
as youth in Boston,
19–25

zoot suit, 24–25

Credits

Photos

Cover photo by UPI/Bettmann

© Bob Adelman/Magnum Photos, Inc., 67

AP/Wide World Photos, 8, 13, 30, 32, 44, 52 (top), 55 (top), 61, 74, 81, 83, 96

© Eve Arnold/Magnum Photos, Inc., 43, 49, 59, 62, 77, 99

The Bettmann Archive, 10, 11 (bottom), 51

Courtesy of the Bostonian Society Old State House, 23

Culver Pictures, 11 (top), 17, 26, 27, 28

FPG International, 25

Paul Fusco/Magnum Photos, Inc., 95

© Charles Gatewood/Magnum Photos, Inc., 93

Historical Pictures/Stock Montage, 37

© Hiroji Kubota/Magnum Photos, Inc., 92

Lansing Public Library, 15

Library of Congress, 66

© John Launois/Black Star, 48 (both), 73

© Dan McCoy/Black Star, 52 (bottom)

© Susan Meiselas/Magnum Photos, Inc., 9

© Charles Moore/Black Star, 60

© Eli Reed/Magnum Photos, Inc., 91

Reuters/Bettmann, 94

UPI/Bettmann, 16, 35, 39, 41, 46, 50, 55 (bottom), 58, 69, 71, 72, 79, 80, 82, 84, 85, 86, 87, 88

© Fred Ward/Black Star, 57

© Dan Weiner/Magnum Photos, Inc., 53

Text

Permission to quote from the following copyrighted material is gratefully acknowledged: Excerpts of "Malcolm X" by Mark Whitaker et al. From *Newsweek*, November 11, 1992, pages 70-72. Copyright 1992, Newsweek, Inc. All rights reserved. Reprinted by permission. Excerpts of Ossie Davis's eulogy of Malcolm X are reprinted by permission of Mr. Davis. Excerpts of Janice Simpson's interview with Spike Lee, "Words with Spike," *Time*, November 23, 1992. Copyright 1992, Time Inc. Reprinted by permission. R. Lee Sullivan, "Spike Lee Versus Mrs. Malcolm X," excerpted by permission of *Forbes* magazine, October 12, 1992, © Forbes Inc., 1992. Excerpts from Bruce Perry's *Malcolm: The Life of a Man Who Changed Black America* are reprinted by permission of Station Hill Press, Inc. Excerpts of Martin Luther King Jr.'s "I Have a Dream" speech courtesy of Mrs. Coretta Scott King.

About the Author

Roger Barr is the author of books on the Vietnam war, Richard Nixon, and radios for Lucent Books in San Diego. His novel *The Treasure Hunt* was published in 1992 by Medallion Press, St. Paul, Minnesota.